HAMLET IN ANALYSIS

HAMLET IN ANALYSIS

Horatio's Story—A Trial of Faith

Meg Harris Williams

THE HARRIS MELTZER TRUST

First published in 1997 by Karnac Books as *A Trial of Faith: Horatio's Story – Hamlet in Analysis*.

Revised edition published in 2014 for The Harris Meltzer Trust by Karnac Books Ltd.

Reissued in 2020 by The Harris Meltzer Trust
60 New Caledonian Wharf
London SE16 7TW

Copyright © 1997, 2014 Meg Harris Williams

The right of Meg Harris Williams to be identified as the author of this work has been asserted in accordance with §§ 77 and 78 of the Copyright Design and Patent Act 1988.

All rights reserved. No part of this publication may be reproduced, stored in a retrieval system, or transmitted, in any form or by any means, electronic, mechanical, photocopying, recording, or otherwise, without the prior written permission of the publisher.

British Library Cataloguing in Publication Data
A C.I.P. for this book is available from the British Library

ISBN 978 1 912567 69 0

Edited, designed and produced by The Bourne Studios
www.bournestudios.co.uk
Printed in Great Britain

www.harris-meltzer-trust.org.uk

I passed the small theater where I once saw a traveling company perform *Hamlet* and remembered how I felt sorry for myself for the way I'd suffered like him ... I was so moved by the play because so much of it was about me and my gloomy life that I dropped sixpence into the lard tin and wished I could have attached a note to let Hamlet know who I was and how my suffering was real and not just in a play.

Frank McCourt, *Teacher Man*

CONTENTS

	About the author	ix
	Foreword to the new edition	xi
	Introduction: Hamlet *as a Dream-play*	1
	Cast of characters	29
1	The Prelude	31
2	The Ghost	51
3	The Prince	65
4	The Mousetrap	81
5	The Grave	97
6	The Winter's Tale	113
7	The Tempest	125

8	*The King and Queen*	139
9	*Ophelia at Colonus*	157
10	*Becoming Fortinbras*	173
11	*Horacio Agonistes*	189
	Index to dreams	203

ABOUT THE AUTHOR

Meg Harris Williams is a visual artist and a literary critic, writing about the relation between psychoanalysis, aesthetics and literature, especially poetry. She has published many papers in psychoanalytic and academic journals and is author and editor of many books. Her authored books are: *Inspiration in Milton and Keats* (1982), *A Strange Way of Killing: the Poetic Structure of Wuthering Heights* (1987), *The Apprehension of Beauty: the Role of Aesthetic Conflict in Development, Art and Violence* (with Donald Meltzer, 1988), *The Chamber of Maiden Thought: Literary Origins of the Psychoanalytic Model of the Mind* (with Margot Waddell; 1991), *Five Tales from Shakespeare* (for children; 1996), *The Vale of Soulmaking: the Post-Kleinian Model of the Mind* (2005), *The Aesthetic Development: the Poetic Spirit of Psychoanalysis* (2010) *Bion's Dream: a Reading of the Autobiographies* (2010), and *The Art of Personality* (2017). She is a visiting lecturer at the Tavistock Clinic and also teaches widely abroad. Many papers and book chapters have been translated into other languages, including Italian, French, German, Spanish, Portuguese, Greek, and Japanese. Website: www.artlit.info.

FOREWORD TO THE NEW EDITION

This novel, originally entitled *A Trial of Faith,* is an exploration of Shakespeare's *Hamlet* in the form of a novel tracing the course of a Kleinian analysis. It is an experiment in literary criticism as much as in fiction, and was written in collaboration with the psychoanalyst Donald Meltzer, who supervised each weekly chapter as it was written, from an analyst's perspective. The intention was to be faithful to the psychoanalytic process as well as to the aesthetic implications of Shakespeare's play.

The narrator and analyst is Horatio, whom Hamlet in the play asks to "tell his story" – the story of an adolescent breakdown. Hamlet as a character invites an unusually close form of identification: as Hazlitt put it, "It is *we* who are Hamlet." Horatio's countertransference as one who is supposed to "suffer all yet suffer nothing" places him in a vulnerable and testing situation that tempts him towards breaches of technique.

The novel, like the play (in my view) is structured around a series of dreams that Hamlet recounts to Horatio. Meanwhile the underlying preoccupation with playing-as-reality highlights some intriguing implications of Shakespeare's own mid-career struggles as a dramatist: concerning the relation between genre, analysand-protagonist and analyst-playwright.

The present revised edition of the novel includes a new introduction, some minor changes to the text, and the insertion of more quotations to mark the source of the emotional conflict. Such markers also illustrate the dreamlike and turbulent reading process of writing literary criticism, which entails not the deconstruction but (as was said of Ophelia) the "unshaping" of language in a way that "botches up words to fit the hearer's own thoughts". It is for readers to judge whether or not the current botching speaks to their own feelings stirred by Shakespeare's play and helps to make sense of the reactions aroused in we who are Hamlet.

INTRODUCTION

Hamlet as a Dream-play

The "Process" into fiction

This book was written in collaboration with Donald Meltzer, with a double objective: on the one hand, to try to put his description of the psychoanalytic process into a modern fiction;[i] on the other, to demonstrate how Shakespeare's play itself fictionalizes a psychoanalytic process. This is possible only because the play as an aesthetic entity invites it: a possibility that suggested itself to me after writing an account of the play's concern with "aesthetic conflict".[ii] *Hamlet* gives us Shakespeare at a watershed in his career, in terms of both his search for a hero, and his development of the genre of the dream-play that began in *A Midsummer Night's Dream*. In this introduction I would like to consider *Hamlet* as a dream-play in which Hamlet as analysand relates his dreams to Horatio as analyst.

---

i D. Meltzer, *The Psychoanalytical Process,* 1967 (reprinted Clunie Press, 1970; Harris Meltzer Trust, 2008).
ii "The undiscovered country" in *The Apprehension of Beauty* (Clunie Press, 1987; reprinted Harris Meltzer Trust, 2008).

Hamlet is Shakespeare's archetypal exploration of the multiple different worlds of adolescence, with its confusion between thought and action, intrusiveness and intimacy – the drama between the inside and outside of the object, and how the adolescent rocks back and forth in constant instability, in and out of the adult world[i]. The play was written in between *Julius Caesar* and *Antony and Cleopatra*, so shows us how Shakespeare's investigation into the qualities of a hero was proceeding between those two plays: "hero" meaning a personality capable of development, capable of becoming itself. With Hamlet, Shakespeare tries a different approach from that in earlier plays: he looks for a hero who can dream, and who tries to think through his dreams. Invariably we identify closely with Hamlet, probably more than any other single character in classic literature, other than perhaps Oedipus himself. However it is not his already formed character that we identify with, but rather, his hopeful potential: his interesting condition of both mourning a lost father, and of being on the verge of falling in love, with all the oedipal emotionality thereby stirred up. And of course, his poetic dreams.

Shakespeare's play is an exploration not just of a particular character but of a new genre in playwriting. They take place simultaneously; this is why the play is almost unplayable, as it is far too long, and is usually shortened for the stage. What is particularly important in the structure of the play is the role of Horatio, who has little to say, yet maintains a presence at all the significant points. Hamlet describes him as the ideal observer – as "one who in suffering all, suffers nothing" (III. ii. 60).[ii] He allows the characters to dream and notes down what he sees. ("Didst perceive?" says Hamlet; "I did very well note", replies Horatio [III. ii. 281-4]). Like the playwright himself, he is intimately identified with, and yet distanced from, their emotional trials. His job is to weave them together into a meaningful symbol, and this, as Hamlet sees, is a type of "suffering" also. There is a sense in which the story is created by the dialogue between Hamlet and

---

i D. Meltzer & M. Harris, *Adolescence: Talks and Papers by Donald Meltzer and Martha Harris,* ed. M. H. Williams (Harris Meltzer Trust, 2011).
ii References to *Hamlet* are to the second Arden edition by H. Jenkins (Methuen, 1982).

Horatio, even though one has many words and the other very few. All Hamlet's "acting", real and unreal, is undertaken with Horatio at the back of his mind, and by the end of the play Horatio has a story of his own to tell, as is made clear when Hamlet insists at the end that he remain alive "to tell [my] story" after his own struggle is ended (V. ii. 347) – literally a narrative transference. Horatio is like the playwright or the psychoanalyst, seeking a container for the dreams that he hears, rather than the plot that he follows.

Although there are many dreams and dreamlike sequences in Shakespeare, *Hamlet* is his first dream-play in the sense of telling an entire story through dreams. Although the characters give a very realistic sense of family relationships, almost like a novel, the events of the plot are patently absurd – the ghost, the pirate ship etc – and a large portion of the centre of the play is taken up with the analysis of acting as an art form, another fictional mode of existence which may or may not symbolize the truth about ourselves and our emotional situation. Is this kind of dream true, or not? As the ancient Greeks might have put it, does it arrive through the gate of horn or of ivory?

As an adolescent, like all adolescents, Hamlet is engaged in a search for the "undiscovered country" of his future self, the new shape of his mind as it might be after the catastrophic change of adolescence. His quest is not entirely successful, at least, not in this play; though we might say Shakespeare takes it up and continues it in subsequent plays. But in no other play does the playwright, or the audience, have the same intense adhesive identification with the hero – as Hazlitt said, "It is *we* who are Hamlet." We inherit this close identification from Shakespeare himself. This might be considered one of the play's problems: a problem that would be understood psychoanalytically in terms of countertransference interference, as not achieving a sufficiently objective viewpoint, but overloading the analysand with expectations. Denmark is described as "sick". As the great hope of the state to which he is heir – soldier, scholar, statesman, "Th'expectancy and rose of the fair state" (III. i. 152) – this prince, a mere adolescent, is expected to reform everybody else's murky emotional problems and disappointments. Marriage with

Ophelia would fulfil what Bion denotes the "messianic" basic assumption of the surrounding group, and create a "new heaven, new earth" – the Biblical phrase which finally attains credence not here but in *Antony and Cleopatra.*

If, as Martha Harris has put it, "the central task of the adolescent is to find identity",[i] this is Hamlet's task – indeed in the first half of the play, his burning desire. He wants to penetrate the difference between "is and "seems", "For I have that within which passes show/ These but the trappings and the suits of woe" (I. ii. 85-56). He wants not to act (as in "actions that a man might play"), but to *be* (as in, becoming himself). He wants to know the "heart of [his] mystery" (III. ii. 330), and is overwhelmed by the aesthetic conflict this entails in his attitude to "the world", its beauty and ugliness. As he phrases it:

> What a piece of work is a man, how noble in reason, how infinite in faculties, in form and moving how express and admirable, in action how like an angel, in apprehension how like a god! The beauty of the world, the paragon of animals – and yet, to me, what is this quintessence of dust? (II. ii. 303-12)

By contrast, his statement near the end of the play that "to know a man well were to know himself" (V. ii. 140) is delivered offhandedly, like a language game, devoid of emotionality. By then he has given up trying to find meaning in the "quintessence of dust". During the second half of the play we feel that Shakespeare has lost interest in him, and the hero's role is taken over by Ophelia, whose existence takes on an absent (mad) or ghostly (dead) quality in Hamlet's mind's eye.

The Ghost dream

The encounter with the Ghost that constitutes Hamlet's first powerful dream brings to light the complexity of his emotional ambivalence, dredged up from the deep unconscious that is symbolized by the space underneath the stage – the "cellarage" – where the Ghost resides, like a mole burrowing "in the

---

[i] Martha Harris, *Your Teenager,* 1969 (new edition, Harris Meltzer Trust, 2007), p. 237.

earth" (I.v.165). This is the context in which Hamlet calls on Horatio's help; indeed Horatio, with the aid of the soldiers on watch (his inner eyes) sees the Ghost before Hamlet and brings him to Hamlet's attention. Deploying Freud's organ of attention (consciousness), he foresees an "eruption in the state of Denmark", whilst hoping at first that the appearance of the Ghost may be just "a mote to trouble the mind's eye" (I. i.111) – words echoed by Hamlet himself, rather to Horatio's surprise, when he tells him he can see his father at that very moment "in [his] mind's eye" (I. ii. 185).

The mind's eye is indeed the place where it all happens. To all the other characters, the Ghost is invisible; and indeed will only speak to Hamlet, even though Horatio is termed a "scholar" – someone who knows about how to speak to ghosts – about which there were definite opinions in Shakespeare's day, just as there are today amongst psychoanalysts, and speaking to ghosts was considered quite a science. Hamlet's plea to the Ghost is "Let me not burst in ignorance" (I.iv.50). He means, not solely ignorance of the Ghost's story, but ignorance of his inner self, which is his essential or core anguish. The Ghost is an internal figure projecting into his son a dream of his own, in which milk was turned into poison by his mother-wife and poured through his ears:

> Sleeping within my orchard,
> My custom always of the afternoon,
> Upon my secure hour thy uncle stole
> With juice of cursed hebenon in a vial,
> And in the porches of my ears did pour
> The leperous distilment, whose effect
> Holds such an enmity with blood of man
> That swift as quicksilver it courses through
> The natural gates and alleys of the body,
> And with a sudden vigour it doth posset
> And curd, like eager droppings into milk,
> The thin and wholesome blood. So did it mine. (I. v. 59-70)

The dream of the Ghost makes clear Hamlet's claustrophobic state and near-schizophrenic delusion that his father is his uncle. The internal father lost in a kind of hellish limbo evokes his ambivalence, becoming the "uncle-father" he calls Claudius.

A childhood idealization of a godlike and heroic figure who could defend his country by means of single-handed duels, has switched to his current disillusion with Claudius' middle-aged decay, depression ("limed soul"), and over-indulgence in sensual pleasures. The two images compare as "Hyperion to a satyr" in his mind. It becomes clear that this ambivalence is rooted in his distrust of hidden, invisible feminine treachery and false "beautified" appearances in his mother and Ophelia. The Ghost claims the milky food of his mind has been poisoned by treachery (I. v. 45-85) and passes this feeling onto Hamlet, inciting him to revenge, whilst at the same time warning him not to "taint his mind or harm his mother" (I. v. 85).

These are contradictory demands of his internal object, and Hamlet reacts ambiguously: he is prompted to act out his vengeance, and at the same time to seek a receiver for his dreams – as is suggested by his wanting to write down his feelings. As Meltzer has said of the adolescent, he is stimulated to go forwards and backwards at the same time. The encounter with the Ghost ends with Hamlet trying to find a container for his emotional disturbance, and implying that Horatio will not be able to do it because it goes beyond his "philosophy" – his existing knowledge about the mind. It is a venture into the unknown reaches of his personality and its internal objects:

> There are more things in heaven and earth, Horatio,
> Than are dreamt of in your philosophy.
> But come,
> Here as before, never, so help you mercy,
> How strange or odd some'er I bear myself –
> As I perchance hereafter shall think meet
> To put an antic disposition on – ... (I. v. 174-80)

The "antic disposition" which he adopts – his "madness" – becomes both a cover for the verbal acting-out that follows, and his aesthetic self-expression. Polonius points this out when later he admiringly says that madness is often nearer the truth than sanity. This artificial madness is not however a true symbol of Hamlet's inner "mystery"; it has the sense of a temporary refuge whilst awaiting further developments.

And Horatio, too, in his countertransference role, needs to deepen his philosophy in order to match or receive Hamlet's communications, which take the form of both communicative and evacuative projections. His state and age is ambiguous – is he a fellow-student, a "good lad" like Rosencrantz and Guildenstern (he knows Hamlet from Wittenberg), or one of the older generation (he remembers old Hamlet)? There is an implication of almost imperceptibly lower social status ("Why should the poor be flatter'd?", III. ii. 59), yet he is seen by the royal family as a measure of disinterested sanity. Our glimpses of Horatio's perspective are few but telling; and it is not Hamlet alone but his entire family with whom he feels involved. When we consider Horatio's role therefore, we may see an analogy not only with that of the dramatist and his multiple identifications, but with the psychoanalyst and his state of mind – the "psychoanalytic attitude" as described by Meltzer in *The Psychoanalytical Process*:

> We must turn our attention to the fundamental unit of the setting, the state of mind of the analyst, and explore the various aspects that are embodied in the concept, the *psycho-analytic attitude*. (*The Psychoanalytical Process*, 1970 [1967], p. 79)

The maintenance of the analyst's state of mind, his "attitude", in "race-horse condition", depends on the interaction of two factors: "scientific curiosity and devotion to method". The challenge for Horatio is not to load Hamlet with his own expectations, making a hero of him through moral improvement (therapeutic zeal); correct interpretation in itself is ineffectual, as Hamlet's impervious reactions to his ironic interjections demonstrate.

The madman dream

Hamlet feels the Ghost-as-internal-father has projected its madness into him, and this stimulates an intrusive attitude towards Ophelia. His next dream is received or "remembered" by Ophelia like the "sins" he later hopes she will contain. It conveys his appearance in her "closet" or private room, half undressed like a traditional caricature of a madman, looking as if, like the Ghost, he had just been released from hell "to speak of horrors":

> **Ophelia**: My lord, as I was sewing in my closet,
> Lord Hamlet, with his doublet all unbrac'd,
> No hat upon his head, his stockings foul'd,
> Ungarter'd and down-gyved to his ankle,
> Pale as his shirt, his knees knocking each other,
> And with a look so piteous in purport
> As if he had been loosed out of hell
> To speak of horrors, he comes before me.
> **Polonius**: Mad for thy love?
> **Ophelia**: My lord, I do not know,
> But truly I do fear it. (II. i. 77-86)

Ophelia says Hamlet gazes on her face, unspeaking, "as if he would draw it". This is in response to Polonius' interference with their relationship – Polonius having told Ophelia to deny Hamlet access to her because his motivation was bound to be dishonourable. Then her obedience is taken by Hamlet as a masochistic passivity – this is how he "draws her face" in his mind, his non-verbal interpretation. It is a kind of "dumb-show" that is repeated later with the play-within-a-play, when the actors mime a nonspeaking prelude to the violent drama to come. The "closet" may represent literally her body, or her mental ambience, her mind. The spirit of vengeance is inextricable from a false aesthetics, introduced into the space by Hamlet himself. This episode is a prelude to the later similar scene in which Hamlet tells Ophelia to go to a nunnery to conceal the falseness of her beauty.

Polonius, to whom this episode is related, is excited by his half-understanding of the problem: "Mad for thy love?" He then uses Ophelia as a tool to investigate Hamlet's mystery, and the paternal transference becomes mixed up with a preconception about Ophelia and her supposed passivity.

It is important to remember that Polonius is a great admirer of Hamlet and in a sense yet another father – the one who has nurtured his intellect and interests such as philosophy and theatre. He is not to be dismissed as only a senile old fool who talks too much. He is the court counsellor but, as with Horatio, Hamlet's state of mind goes beyond the reach of his existing philosophy. Although he is a comic character, his advice is good and the content of his interpretations is correct; but it has bad results, owing to his unaesthetic *methods* of investigation, which stimulate action rather than contemplation. His attitude to both Hamlet and his son Laertes is circuitous to the point of dishonesty – as in the instruction to "by indirections find directions out" (II. i. 66). He tries to "spy out where truth is hid", treating Hamlet's inner mystery as if it were a riddle to be solved:

> I will find
> Where truth is hid, though it were hid indeed
> Within the centre. (II.ii.149-51)

He wants to hunt down the quarry, rather than receive symbolically its meaning. Consequently Hamlet complains justly that all the court – the adult world – want to "pluck out the heart of my mystery", his internal Ghost. Polonius is oblivious to the fact that the means are essential to the end – and as Bion points out in another context, those who disregard the means are following the path to the Sirens and will end up with nothing but a pile of old bones.

At the same time, and by a further analogy, Shakespeare uses Polonius as a way of criticizing certain temptations which the playwright is subject to: the dramatist who is seduced by his own virtuosity and who takes a directorial role, determined that everything shall fall out as planned. These inhibiting and omnipotent attitudes become clear during the fiasco of the Mousetrap, the play-within-a-play. In later plays this type of character appears as the Prospero-wizard in *The Tempest* or the Duke of *Measure for Measure*. The dominating, controlling mentality does not help the adolescent who is concerned with the difference between "being" and "playing". As he says to his mother, it is not his outward appearance and gestures (the "forms, moods, shapes of grief") that can "denote [him] truly":

> For I have that within which passeth show
> These but the trappings and the suits of woe. (I. ii. 82-6)

His clothes and body echo his mental state, as with the typical adolescent, but they are not the same thing as his inner "grief" which neither he nor they understand. The result of the Madman Dream is not just to confirm Hamlet's disturbance, but to demonstrate how this is increased by the adult world's messianic expectations of the young couple. The adults are as much responsible as Hamlet for creating an anti-aesthetic container for emotional trouble, that strangles personality development. They hope Hamlet will rescue them from their middle-aged sloppiness, drinking etc; but allow him no space to do so. He says truly that Denmark is a "prison", represented by the way he feels confined within the Lobby, a corridor with windows from which the sky is just visible, and where he paces up and down reading "words, words, words", full of emptiness (II. ii. 184).

The Mousetrap dream

Although *Hamlet* is traditionally seen as a play in which the hero thinks too much and cannot act, in fact the opposite is the case. Hamlet's danger is in thinking too little and acting too precipitously – it just happens that because of his verbal virtuosity, his actions often take the form of words, speeches and cutting remarks. Acting-out can be verbal or visual; it is not the medium that makes the difference, but the way it is used – for exploration or for evacuation of the emotional conflict, for or against knowledge (K or –K in Bion's formula).

This is the drama of the Mousetrap – which again may be seen as an extended, enacted symbol of Hamlet's contempt for the nature of his ageing parents' sexuality and the "sick soul" which he has truly glimpsed in both Gertrude and Claudius (IV. v. 17; III. iii. 85). It is at the centre of the play and knots together its various contradictory, conflictual strands of meaning, trying to define the adolescent condition that has become trapped by its own dreams.

The performance of the Mousetrap itself is preceded by the long investigation into the nature of acting as an art-form, conducted by Hamlet, Polonius and the Players; and by the "nunnery" scene with Ophelia (III.i). The sequences about acting might appear to be a digression, but if we remember that the nature of aesthetic conflict lies at the heart of the play, then acting as an art form becomes central to how plays are conducted, and to the question of whether they are truth-revealing or truth-obscuring, for both the viewers and the participants. It is Hamlet who gives the play-within-a-play the title "Mousetrap", indicating that he is well aware it is not produced for truthful purposes but in order to impose a meaning which he has preconceived – namely, a lie. It is not necessarily a lie about external facts or events, but a lie about their meaning in the soul. In fact we are no longer interested in the original question posed by the plot, namely did Claudius kill old Hamlet or not, and was Gertrude an accomplice. Once we understand the dream-like structure of the entire play, it is clear that these are subjective matters of the adolescent's changing attitude to his parents, and their puzzled but guilty reactions to his state of mind – far more interesting than objective matters of plot.

The scenes with the Players are significant not just for their investigation of the theme of truthful symbol-formation based on aesthetic reciprocity (as can happen – but may not happen – with actors and audience); they are also significant for their presentation of Hamlet's schooldays and his former relationship with Polonius, which was clearly based on a mutual infatuation with acting as an art form – with words, their presentation, their effect on a listener. In this situation the play is itself the aesthetic object. What is the actor doing inside it – is his position intrusive or demonstrative? What sort of transference goes on when the actor becomes vehicle for an idea?

> What's he to Hecuba, or Hecuba to him,
> That he should weep for her? (II. ii. 518-19)

asks Hamlet, questioning the authenticity of the actor's emotion, and hence his own, in directing the Mousetrap. He takes it upon himself to "reform" the actors' art: "Suit the action to the word, the word to the action" he instructs the Player, in the identical manner to Polonius (III.ii.16). The actor is a vehicle for feelings which are distinct from his own person. When do they tell the truth about a situation, and when are they a lie?

Obsessed by these distinctions and unable to find a truthful answer to his inner confusion, Hamlet as before projects them onto Ophelia in the nunnery scene. Ophelia enters at a critical moment after Hamlet has been trying to authentically contain his emotional anxiety in the "To be or not to be" soliloquy, attempting to transcend his contempt for his family members by means of an abstract questioning of life and death:

> To die – to sleep,
> No more; and by a sleep to say we end
> The heart-ache and the thousand natural shocks
> That flesh is heir to: 'tis a consummation
> Devoutly to be wish'd. To die, to sleep;
> To sleep, perchance to dream – ay, there's the rub;
> For in that sleep of death what dreams may come,
> When we have shuffled off this mortal coil,
> Must give us pause… (III. i. 60-68)

In this speech he considers the possibility of replacing action ("resolution") by the pale and sickly colouring of thought; it is the "pause" in his manic rush towards revenge:

> And thus the native hue of resolution
> Is sicklied o'er with the pale cast of thought,
> And enterprises of great pitch and moment
> With this regard their currents turn awry
> And lose the name of action. Soft you now,
> The fair Ophelia! Nymph, in thy orisons
> Be all my sins remember'd. (III. i. 84-90)

Ophelia's entry at this point brings him back to earth – to the kind of dream that undermines abstract philosophical speculation and anchors him back in the messy emotionality of his "madness", which has become further complicated by Polonius and his directorial manoeuvres designed to expose the root of Hamlet's madness. In this false kind of play, Ophelia – like his college friends Rosencrantz and Guildenstern – is a tool, as Hamlet very soon suspects: "Where's your father?" he demands (l. 130), sensing his presence hidden behind a pillar in the Lobby – an intruder in his dream-space, his internal mother, just as he will be when he hides behind the arras (tapestry curtain) in Gertrude's chamber, making it a claustral compartment in Meltzer's sense.

The consequence of Hamlet's misinterpretation of Ophelia's own life-space means that, in his view, she becomes a traitor to aesthetic values:

> Get thee to a nunnery…. I have heard of your paintings well enough. God hath given you one face and you make yourselves another… it hath made me mad. I say we will have no more marriage. (III. i. 137-149)

She becomes in his eyes a puppet manipulated from within by the domineering aspect of Polonius to which he is allergic, all the more since it is also an aspect of himself. Obedient to Polonius' instructions, she returns the various gifts and poems Hamlet has given her. This offends Hamlet not just because she is Polonius' agent rather than acting of her own volition, but because he (like Polonius) believes his poems are no good, and this is a critical but objective judgement on his own literary failure. All these pile up together in the way he experiences Ophelia's rejection. After this Hamlet gives up the apparently impossible business of thinking through his emotional ambivalence to all his friends and family, but particularly his mother and Ophelia. He gives over the struggle to nurture the embryonic, fragile "pale cast of thought", and abandons himself to revenge, destroying the very possibility of any authentic emotional link – "no more marriage". Hence while the Mousetrap is playing in front of the assembled court, Hamlet provides a commentary of pornographic word-play while he lies with his head on Ophelia's lap. This stance, at the front of the stage, colours the Players' performance as seen by the rest of the court. He is deliberately converting the story into a symbol of sexual perversion. The actors, like Ophelia, are manipulated to suit his fantasy of a tainted beauty ("face") which disguises an ulcerated secret, a false coition. So after the dumb-show, which enacts a poisoning, Ophelia asks Hamlet what this "show" meant; and his interpretation is redirected toward her: "Be not you ashamed to show, he'll not shame to tell you what it means" (III. ii. 140).

> **Hamlet**: It would cost you a groaning to take off my edge.
> **Ophelia**: Still better, and worse.
> **Hamlet**: So you mis-take your husbands. – Begin, murderer. Leave thy damnable faces and begin. Come, the croaking raven doth bellow for revenge. (III. ii. 244-49)

The pun on "taking" (sexually, and semantically) indicates that husbands and wives are a "mis-take"; what is desired is revenge on the whole idea of marriage.

The only exception to this anti-aesthetic or manic mode occurs in the brief private conversations with Horatio, just before and just after the Mousetrap itself. Beforehand, Hamlet takes Horatio aside and tells him that for him, he has been

> As one in suff'ring all, that suffers nothing...
> Give me that man
> That is not passion's slave, and I will wear him
> In my heart's core, ay in my heart of heart,
> As I do thee. (III. ii. 66-74)

Afterwards, Horatio with gentle sarcasm tries to defuse his triumph at the chaos caused by the Mousetrap. The idea of a type of suffering that is in a sense not personally generated is an apt description of the countertransference. But these moments of near-communication do not have any impact, because Hamlet has in a sense seduced Horatio through a kind of princely tolerance; Horatio in his psychoanalytic capacity is de-skilled and cannot penetrate Hamlet's mania. This is a further triumph for the manic side of Hamlet, and leads directly to the scene with his mother in her closet, echoing that earlier with Ophelia, in which he kills Polonius by blindly stabbing him as he hides behind the curtains. It doesn't make much difference whether it is the king (as he first thinks) or Polonius. It is a phallic intruder – a "rat", a penis-mouse confused with a baby – the intruding male who is also an aspect of himself, stage-managing the inner spaces of his mother:

> Thou wretched, rash, intruding fool, farewell. (III. iv. 31).

The interview then becomes dominated by another intruding fool – by Hamlet's "wagging tongue" as Gertrude calls it:

> What have I done, that thou dar'st wag thy tongue
> In noise so rude against me? (III. iv. 39)

When the Ghost reappears, she cannot see it; her incomprehension of what is inside Hamlet reinforces his isolation. The Ghost almost inspires a change of heart in Hamlet, talking of "tears" instead of "blood", but the Queen's blindness means that no such emotional link is achieved. This scene is the culmination of the vengeful action that has been coming to a crescendo throughout the first half of the play, with Horatio helplessly looking on, but failing in any way to contain Hamlet's mania, owing to the seductive force of this particular adolescent's qualities – the potential soldier, scholar, statesman, actor, philosopher, and lover that everybody can see in him, and that never comes to fruition. It all ends in the disaster imaged by the stage strewn with corpses – the "accidental judgements, casual slaughters" of the final scene.

But meanwhile the second half of the play is given to Ophelia and the female voice, while Hamlet is away on his sea-voyage, dreaming about pirates and conspiracies, taking revenge on the foolish friends he has outwitted. The price for being the Prince is to be an only child.

The dream of Ophelia's madness

During Acts IV and V Shakespeare seems to put his interest in Hamlet aside, as if he needs him out of the way in order to concentrate properly on the feminine aspects of this adolescent disturbance.

The dream of Ophelia's madness is really a dream that Horatio has on behalf of Hamlet. The King appoints him to "watch" Ophelia – to become her special observer. In literal terms of the plot, Horatio makes a very bad guard, since Ophelia then goes and drowns herself – and not only this, but she appears to have done it in full view of the Queen. At least, this is what the vividness of the Queen's narrative of the drowning appears to evoke. The drowning is thus Horatio's dream of Gertrude's dream of Ophelia's internal preoccupations. All this goes to emphasize the extent to which *Hamlet* has become a dream play, not an ordinary revenge tragedy. In this section the women come to the fore and express their feelings in a different kind of symbolic language.

Shakespeare's most recent heroines, Viola and Rosalind, escape the conventional confines of their sex by dressing as men. In the case of Ophelia, Shakespeare tries another method, using dream instead of disguise as a means of self-expression. Ophelia brings in the idea of a different type of symbol-seeking, one in which words – in the sense of explanations – have little use. In the Mousetrap scene she said to Hamlet, "I think nothing", meaning, she did not want to collude in his dirty thoughts, contain his "sins". Nonetheless she has taken them in and digested them in an idiosyncratic way. She seems retiring and over-obedient at first, as though still stuck in latency. Yet when pushed to the point she shows she has more resilience in a sexual relationship than either Hamlet or Laertes. Earlier when Laertes tried to lecture her on how to behave with Hamlet she made a spirited if quiet response, reminding him to concentrate on managing himself (I.iii.45). Possibly because she is not encumbered with the same career expectations as the boys, she can quietly develop more of a private mental space. The world of her mind and imagination only becomes evident through her "madness". This is itself an introjection of Hamlet's madness, which Polonius had admired for its "pregnant" verbal vehicle, and which Ophelia now reshapes. It is not however a masochistically received projection, but a reforming mirror.

By this point in the play, "words, words, words" have got a bad name for emptiness, trickiness and game-playing – for manipulation rather than communication. The aesthetic potential of words for emotional communication has been lost. Hamlet's sanctimonious "reforming" of the players' speeches showed how easily art may be turned into pornography under the guise of cleaning up its message.

Ophelia's madness presents an alternative possibility. At first the Queen does not wish to speak to Ophelia, knowing she would find it too painful. The messenger describes the quality of her speech:

> Her speech is nothing,
> Yet the unshaped use of it doth move
> The hearers to collection. They aim at it,
> And botch the words up fit to their own thoughts,
> Which, as her winks and nods and gestures yield them,
> Indeed would make one think there might be thought,
> Though nothing sure, yet much unhappily. (IV.v.4-13)

Her speech is "nothing" and "unshaped" yet it has aesthetic potential – by contrast with Hamlet's view of the glory of the world as a "quintessence of dust"; it moves the listeners to emotional contact and imaginative response. Ultimately it is the Queen who, despite her reluctance, receives Ophelia's communications most intuitively, thereby strengthening the feminine parts of the adolescent self and their capacity for thinking and symbol-formation. "Lord we know what we are, but know not what we may be" (IV. v. 44), philosophizes Ophelia, echoing Hamlet's many queries about adolescent identity. She then sings a "Valentine" song about the loss of virginity:

> And I a maid at your window,
> To be your Valentine.
> Then up he rose, and donn'd his clothes,
> And dupp'd the chamber door,
> Let in the maid that out a maid
> Never departed more. (IV. v. 50-55)

With Ophelia's mad songs, music enters in to the play, having been notably absent (for Shakespeare) till that point. There is a sense in which all poetry seems nonsense, yet it speaks through its music. The mad scenes herald the future shape of the late romance plays with their music-and-water dreamlike quality, and the need to stake all the play's meaning on some "insubstantial pageant". It is the beginning of a search for a new symbolic mode, and a form of restitution for the way the actors and their art were abused in the Mousetrap.

Ophelia's pregnancy is implied by poetic imagery of flowers and water. It is the Queen who picks this up and empathizes with it in the form of her dream of Ophelia's drowning:

> Her clothes spread wide,
> And mermaid-like awhile they bore her up,
> Which time she chanted snatches of old lauds
> As one incapable of her own distress,
> Or like a creature native and indued
> Unto that element. (IV. vii. 174-79)

The drowning represents her flowering as an individual in a kind of quiet rebellion that distances her from the rotting values of the adult world, the court. Realistically, the Queen cannot have been an eye-witness of Ophelia drowning, nor can Horatio. What Horatio notices through his countertransference dream is not an external reality, but an internal one, through identification, in this case with the feminine vertex or dimension. The structure of the play is becoming dream-within-dream.

The Grave dream

The last major dream in *Hamlet* is the Grave dream, the prelude to the final catastrophe when, in effect, Hamlet's personal development is abandoned by the playwright, and Horatio is given the task of re-writing his entire story in another play – or future plays – for the seeds of all Shakespeare's subsequent oeuvre are sown in *Hamlet*. This final dream comprises the premature ending of Hamlet's story, and has three successive movements: the first reawakening a nostalgic longing for his childhood relation with a combined male-female object; the second marking the loss of Ophelia as a feasible relationship; and the third acknowledging the resulting mess made of his life, with the death of all these hopes and potentialities.

Throughout the play Hamlet as a character has been set in a context not just of the adult world – the court – but the world of his own contemporaries, in particular the male adolescent group represented by Rosencrantz and Guildenstern, Laertes, and Fortinbras. The first two he came to regard as traitors in the sense of acting as spies for the king, creatures of the establishment; Laertes he has antagonized owing to his effect on both Polonius and Ophelia (even if we see their "deaths" metaphorically). Fortinbras ("strong arm") remains as a possible route for the adolescent to follow, even though up to this point Hamlet has found him absurd and incomprehensible. The "lawless resolutes" that he "shark'd up" at the beginning of the play comprise a new style of mercenary army, perhaps like Brechtian city-gangsters, slick and affluent. Certainly the type of invasion he embodies seems specially designed to engulf a society that is suffering not from the ravages of war but from "th'imposthume of too much wealth and peace" (IV.iv.27). Claudian prosperity has an internal price, and the changing social climate in both Norway and Denmark is something that the older generation feel to be outside their control. They are tired, and insidiously pressurize Hamlet to repair their own mistakes and metabolize this new dictatorship.

After the confrontation with his mother, Hamlet (in another dream) observes Fortinbras with his entire army marching across the stage, apparently unnoticed by anybody else. Why, he wonders, does the Norwegian prince bother to lead a huge army to conquer a worthless patch of ground, just to make his name – sacrificing life "even for an eggshell":

> Witness this delicate and tender prince,
> Whose spirit with divine ambition puffed
> Makes mouths at the invisible event,
> Exposing what is mortal and unsure
> To all that fortune, death, and danger dare,
> Even for an eggshell. (IV. iv. 48-53)

The adolescent route represented by Fortinbras, the ambitious military adventurer, is that described by Meltzer in terms of the ruthless thrust for success – in any field – that some adolescents retreat into when the dreaminess becomes too painful and makes them feel too helpless. It is really an extended latency and it only shows symptomatically later – from about age 30 – when they become "neurotic". It is the false success that comes from abandoning the struggle with the feminine or emotional side of their nature. Meltzer writes:

> One of the paradoxes of adolescence is precisely this: the adolescent thinks that what leads him forward into the adult world is in reality regressive, while that which he experiences as the thing which pushes him back, to the point of making him into a child again, is in reality the very thing which makes him an adult… What he believes might take him back towards childhood – feelings, emotions, the fascination of childhood itself, of attachment and awareness of the beauty of the world and of his own impotence and weakness – leads him towards the adult world; while the ruthlessness, in reality, prevents him from becoming an adult. The crucial point in his decision whether to go forwards or backwards is the problem of mental suffering: should he be ruthless, inflicting suffering on others in order to achieve success, or should he turn backwards and be the one to suffer?[i]

He adds that "Very rarely do young people come to us [psychoanalysts] who are advancing relentlessly towards success and who have learned how to inflict suffering on others." Yet this seems to be the lesson that Hamlet is trying to learn from Fortinbras, against his better judgement, and against the better nature of the childish self that was truly a "sweet prince". His conclusion, in defiance of his thinking capacity, is that he, like Fortinbras, needs to have "bloody thoughts" or they are "worth nothing" (Bion's –K). It is at precisely this point that Shakespeare abandons Hamlet and turns to Ophelia and her madness.

Fortinbras passes on his way with his army, but his example hovers at the back of Hamlet's mind. Hamlet, after Ophelia's madness, is sent away from the court, supposedly to England where "everyone is as mad as he is" (V. i. 150). In terms of the plot, of course, Hamlet never reaches England, since he returns by jumping onto a pirate ship – another dream, in which he turns his ex-friends Rosencrantz and Guildenstern over to the establishment, to be "killed" in his stead (that is, absorbed into some type of reformatory or respectable career). Earlier, when they questioned him about the nature of his disturbance, he told them sarcastically: "I lack advancement" (III. ii. 331). They

---

i Meltzer in D. Meltzer & M. Harris, *Adolescence: Talks and Papers* (Harris Meltzer Trust, 2011), p. 27.

cannot comprehend the internal claustrophobia which makes Denmark a "prison" in which Hamlet is bounded by his own bad dreams: "Oh God", he exclaimed in a passionate attempt at communication, "I could be bounded in a nutshell and count myself a king of infinite space, were it not that I have bad dreams" (III. ii. 254-56). The question of what is advancement, for the adolescent, lies at the heart of the entire play. Hamlet means he cannot advance his mental progress; they understand him to mean he is not sure he will inherit the kingship.

The separation or split with Ophelia however – the death of their relationship – results in Hamlet giving up the struggle for advancement in the complex psychological sense. He feels he has to pursue some simpler, more predetermined role or identity. He is age 30 when he reappears on Danish soil with the taunting announcement to the King: "High and mighty, you shall know I am set naked on your kingdom" (IV. vii. 41), implying that despite his nakedness, he is ready to take on a battle for the kingship. The following scenes, with the Gravedigger, Ophelia's burial, and the duel with Laertes, are a series of dream-sequences during which he proceeds to transfer his identity to that of Fortinbras the Norwegian.

He is cured of his original form of "madness" by the time he meets the Gravedigger, whom he encounters with Horatio at his side. Horatio, as always, quietly but inefficaciously endeavours to support Hamlet's half-hearted reparative attempts. However the Gravedigger's verbal "equivocation" outmatches Hamlet's earlier wordplay and highlights the fact that this game can only disguise truth not reveal it. At the same time the (partial) truth is in fact turned up, during the conversation, by digging with the spade (an analytic metaphor). The results of this digging shake his equanimity by showing him the ruin of his childlike and his feminine side. He remembers what it was to be a child playing and riding on the back of Yorick the jester or actor (the father of his early childhood); now all that remains is an empty skull, like an empty stage, where once there was a face and lips: "Here hung those lips that I have kissed I know not how oft". The skull turns into "my lady's chamber" – the feminine space – and revolts him: "how abhorred it is". We remember the Nunnery scene when he accused Ophelia of a "painted" beauty whose face disguised a deep ugliness: "You jig and amble, and you lisp, you nickname God's creatures" (III.i.145). In each situation the nature of the ugliness recalls the specific art of acting and the true or false faces of its movements, its language, its scene-painting.

Horatio tries to stop Hamlet's phantasy going entirely down the anal route to Alexander's "bunghole":

> **Hamlet**: Why, may not imagination trace the noble dust of Alexander till a find it stopping a bung-hole?
> **Horatio**: 'Twere to consider too curiously to consider so. (V. i. 19-7).

But his efforts are aborted by the next dream, the one of Ophelia's burial, which is in a sense also the burial of Hamlet's hopes of revitalizing the "sweet prince" that he was was in his childhood. When he leaps into the grave with the words "This is I, Hamlet the Dane" (V. i. 233), it is the status of princeliness that is dominant, even though there is also a hint of authenticity in his declaration that he loved Ophelia. The predominant emotion is still that he cannot endure being "outfaced" by Laertes, implying that his mere brotherliness is a lesser form of love – less earth-shaking and grandiose:

> Dost thou come here to whine,
> To outface me with leaping in her grave?
> Be buried quick with her? – and so will I.
> And if thou prate of mountains let them throw
> Millions of acres on us, till our ground,
> Singeing his pate against the burning zone,
> Make Ossa like a wart! Nay, an thou'lt mouth,
> I'll rant as well as thou. (V. i. 256-63)

His feminine side is buried under "mountains" and his Fortinbras-side takes over the kingdom of his mind, as is represented by his own death and the sudden arrival of Fortinbras to take over the Danish court which has systematically obliterated itself.

By the time of his participation in the King's stage-managed duel with Laertes, Hamlet has given up the struggle to become himself and slipped into his socially predetermined role. Hence the artificiality of his public apology before the duel; he has ceased trying to *express himself*, and has begun, like Claudius and the whole line of "kings" (pillars of society), to cynically *make speeches* – the speeches which society requires of him. He is ready, in fact, to become Fortinbras.

Hamlet's inner poetry returns in his final words, but only because through these he hands his "story" and his thwarted nascent identity over to Horatio, preventing him from drinking from the poisoned cup:

> O God, Horatio, what a wounded name
> Things standing thus unknown, shall I leave behind me.
> If thou didst ever hold me in thy heart,
> Absent thee from felicity awhile,
> And in this harsh world draw thy breath in pain
> To tell my story. (V. ii. 349-54)

Only Horatio is left to try to make sense of Hamlet's story. By the end of *Hamlet,* Shakespeare realizes that his role is not to be in love with any particular character, but with the method – the method of writing plays. From now on he would not try to construct a hero from qualities that he personally admired, such as those embodied in Brutus, but simply follow the dreams presented to him by the entire cast of characters whom he would observe with evenly suspended attention, in the way later advocated in the use of the psychoanalytic method.

The psychoanalytic process as aesthetic object

The final chapter of this book is concerned with Horatio's review of his emotional involvement in Hamlet's story and the possible analytic mistakes that he made as a result. The paragraphs specifically relating to this were written by Donald Meltzer as a basis for the chapter. In his elaboration of the "psychoanalytic attitude" in books from the *Psychoanalytic Process* onwards, Meltzer stresses the fact that the successful operation of the transference depends on the analytic not the personal qualities of the analyst – that is, his ability to "preside over the psychoanalytic process" – and how, in turn, this generates a sense of the analytic process as itself an aesthetic object, in the eyes of both patient and analyst. Ultimately it is this mutual dedication to the aesthetics of the method that allows the "natural history" of the transference relationship to unfold in logical stages of evolution through a conversation between internal objects.

In Meltzer's view, Horatio loses Hamlet (Hamlet "dies") not because of the intrinsic difficulties of the analysis, but because he fails to faithfully follow the psychoanalytic method. He appears to be following it, but self-examination afterwards illuminates points at which he lost his tolerance, his capacity for negative capability – for the special "suffering" appropriate to the conditions of psychoanalysis. It is a "trial of faith" because he puts his faith – really his expectations – into the patient rather than into the method, and hopes to mould Hamlet accordingly. He is unable to eschew memory and desire, in Bion's terms. Instead, weakened by personal but not unusual problems that are extraneous to the analysis, Horatio is tempted to seek refuge in what appears to be the seductive world of Hamlet's qualities. His attempts to reform their rich potential result in some apparent external success (the easing of symptoms) but in a deeper failure, and he becomes of no use to his patient. Indeed in the play the word "reform" implies patronization, just as the manipulation of "words, words, words" is synonymous with equivocation; both are inimical to symbol-formation and the imaginative investigation of dreams.

The *Process* insists that nothing short of being "in love with" the method can sustain the analyst in a situation of trial, and when love fades, then respect for "the demands of the task" allows his usefulness to continue. The price paid by Horatio in the novel involves the loss of not only Hamlet but of his wife and family as well – costing not less than everything as the poet put it. Feeling this loss on the pulses, he then triumphs in the sense of learning from experience; his failures, reviewed and understood, enable him to develop as a psychoanalyst. Similarly, Shakespeare's own turbulence and love-hate relationship with the process of playing-and-writing lies at the heart of Hamlet's story, expressing his cynicism and despair at the vulnerability of the players as well as his rage at the tyrannical attitudes of the patrons. And the playwright's mind, not just society, contains both players and patrons. The only way out was to go back in again – to become an ass like Bottom, in love with a fairytale. "The play's the thing", an aesthetic object with a life beyond any of its constituents, authors or actors. Writing *Hamlet* gave Shakespeare the inner propulsion which told him it was an absolute necessity to override the previous limits of dramatic form and to allow the dream to become the central, dynamic, organizing feature of a play's structure. Players and patrons then fall into place, as they did in *Midsummer*. On this new or rather newly confirmed basis he wrote the subsequent dream-plays such as *King Lear, The Winter's Tale,* and *The Tempest*.

This novel speculates therefore on an analogy between analyst and playwright that is suggested by the organic concerns that exist within Shakespeare's play. The Meltzerian view places the activity of the psychoanalyst squarely in the tradition of the philosopher-craftsmen from the ancient Greek *demiurge* onwards, weaving the web which will make manifest the meaning of their culture. As Bion put it, "What kind of artists can we be?"[i]

---

i W. R. Bion, *Bion in New York and Sao Paulo* (Clunie Press, 1980), p. 73.

A TRIAL OF FAITH

CAST OF CHARACTERS

Dr David Horacio – a psychoanalyst
Antigone and Ismene Horatio – his daughters

Claude Dane – a wealthy industrializt
Gertrude Dane – his wife
Hamlet Dane – a student at Cambridge University

Professor Antony Polack – a professor of English at Cambridge University
Ophelia Polack – a student at Cambridge University
Nando Polack – her brother

Mrs Forte – a newspaper owner
Forte – her son

Rosenfeld and Gildstein – students, friends of Hamlet

CHAPTER ONE

The Prelude

> O God, Horatio, what a wounded name
> Things standing thus unknown, shall I leave behind me.
> If thou didst ever hold me in thy heart,
> Absent thee from felicity awhile,
> And in this harsh world draw thy breath in pain
> To tell my story. (V. ii. 349-54)

Hamlet, aged 19, commences analysis with Dr Horacio, who recognizes his "uncle-father" delusion and loneliness as an only child.

November 1981. That interesting book by the melancholy young Dane with its grindingly repetitive yet fascinating spirals of sentences lay open where I had left it that Sunday afternoon before taking the dog for his afternoon walk. The small circular table near the window was where I preferred to sit and read. Now it was dusk and it was my custom always to draw the curtains as my narrow, terraced house in Flask Walk, which also contained my consulting room, exposed me to the view of passing patients – many of whom lived locally. As I moved past the table I clumsily jogged my right arm, which was in plaster owing to an absurd accident I had had the previous night, and surprisingly painful. The light from the two tall Georgian windows leapt over the basement chasm and glistened on the wet, narrow, uneven pavement outside (characteristic of the old village of Hampstead). It reached to the place where tree roots pushed the stone upwards. A young woman wearing ugly large trainers strode through the light squares as I closed the curtain, going in the direction of the village. There was a temporary lull in the rainy stormy weather which had been blustering on for the past fortnight, though at the end of the road in the darkness where the massed trees and wide spaces of the Heath began, the energies of the storm still growled with the soughing of branches in the wind.

Since living alone I had become a voracious reader. I imagined Kierkegaard, who had compared himself with Shakespeare's Hamlet, stalking the flat pavements of Copenhagen, pursuing his compulsive strategy of spying on Regine, his Ophelia, in order to wean himself away. (Elsinore too was flat – its cliffs and abysses, drawing into madness, belonged to the topography of the mind, not the earth.) "If I had had faith, I would have stayed with Regine." What a brilliant insight! This was the phrase which had been revolving in my own mind that afternoon as I walked with the dog in the chill soggy air, warming me from within like a glass of claret. And yet, to the casual reader – to one whose hunger for a certain truth had not sharpened his appetite to seize on such a phrase as eager prey – it might (like the "Beauty is Truth" of Keats's *Grecian Urn*) seem a trite commonplace devoid of meaning, a romantic excuse, a capitulation to social acceptability: marriage is good for you.

> In this harsh world draw thy breath in pain
> To tell my story.

Those words, too. It was now eight years since I had had my Hamlet in analysis, though less than a week since I had seen him last. In those eight years society had changed, my personal life had changed, the world had changed, Hamlet had changed from the surly, rebellious young prince who had first enthralled me, and become a pillar of the establishment – not actually a psychoanalyst but what was bad enough, an omnipotent social analyst. Of course I knew very well that patients who fail to regain their lost capacity for passionate experience become either enemies or apostles of psychoanalysis. Lost analysands, lost souls. And the road Hamlet had taken doubtless satisfied any craving he had for apostolic functioning, without being overtly directed against me. But why had he felt the need to take that road at all? Why the urgency, why the weakness? What had happened since that brief but intense period of analysis he had had with me? Broken off prematurely after less than a year, it had lain suspended cocoon-like in my memory, serving – I had always assumed – through the small amount of good we had achieved to keep his insight alive until the moment when he realized he would need to resume. One of those aspects of life that Jung described as glowing coals under grey ashes, lying for years in the lumber-room, waiting to be properly experienced. *Tell my story.* Mine too.

My dog, a huge and elderly Pyrenean mountain dog with long white hair, thumped his tail as he lay down on the Chinese rug and scattered some damp leaves over the beautifully waxed, wide wooden floorboards of my small and elegant sitting room. I had a vivid memory of how ten or twelve years ago in what seemed like another existence, those boards had been covered with a cheap rubber-backed carpet to absorb the noise of the clatterings and shrill clamourings of our two little girls, modulated by the regular admonitions of Beatrice: "*Be quiet!* Daddy's working, down below." A ghost in the cellarage, my consulting room being directly underneath. *A worthy pioner* – no, not a *pioneer*, just a humble mole, an archaeologist of the unconscious. *Canst work in the earth so fast?* How very different were my anxieties about work interference now – how different my worry about my daughters; I was still fulminating over events in the restaurant last night, more in anger than in depression. And how was it that what had once been a joyful love affair with psychoanalysis now seemed to have become an enslavement (workaholism as my daughter called it)? Then for eight years I had been waiting ... for what? for Hamlet's return – for the resumption of our work, which I now saw could never be? The waste, the futility! But why should the history of

Hamlet and his family and friends have so deeply affected me? Feelings and associations had been stirred up during the past week which clustered around this aborted analysis in such a way that it seemed to be coming to represent the focus of my discontent with my life, even the source of my anger with my own family. Was Hamlet a personification of my youthful ambition? He was very different from the type of young man I had been twenty years before him. And I had had analytic "sons" before. True, I had glimmerings of the way in which his relationship with his mother and with Ophelia seemed to mirror, or become confused with, the disintegration of my relationship with my wife. How deeply wounded I had been to discover Beatrice had been unfaithful to me, how angry. I could never have been unfaithful to her. Beatrice, my Regine. She too had changed, like Hamlet, and lost faith in me.

Draw thy breath in pain, he said. I rested my broken arm by the book on the table in the circular light of the table lamp and opened with some difficulty a bottle of red wine, meditating on the possibility that in some way the pain of Hamlet's story was also the pain of my own story. I needed to approach the one through the other in order to make any real headway in understanding my unhappiness. What is faith, after all, but the strength to undergo passionate experience – to approach the unknown, as Kierkegaard said, in "fear and trembling"? My father, the gentle Rabbi, had brought me up in the radiance of his own faith – no refuge for certainties, but exemplifying through spiritual sweetness the tolerance of uncertainties. It was he who warned me:

> The three substitutes
> In love for faith
> Are memory, hope
> And sudden death.

My profession, too, has its credo, its articles of faith. Had I not vowed to receive the fearful strength of the emotion transferred from the patient's internal objects, with all its gross exaggeration of the analyst's attributes, giant- or god-like? And in doing so, to also accept the equal power of the countertransference it evokes: namely the parental responsibility, or sense of responsibility, that enables one to see the child and even the infant in the patient. I had so vowed; this was the article of faith to which I adhered, the prerequisite for the operation of the psychoanalytic imagination. I pondered on some of the wellknown modes of breaking faith with the truth of imagination in my profession – charging exorbitant fees, exalting commonsense, enlisting in the Quality Police, our modern consumerist version of Orwell's Thought Police. I was not, I thought, guilty of these. There were indeed more subtle, more intimate forms of betrayal – evasions, softenings, glossings over the truth. Had there been any such evasions in my handling of Hamlet's analysis, anything that might have contributed to his present regression? I knew I had made mistakes; I had been slow in grasping the significance of his quicksilver changes – characteristic of the adolescent mind. But the method allows for this timelag; by the time a new configuration is understood, it has already appeared many times unobserved. The analyst is, after all, always trailing miles behind the patient's unconscious. Hindsight is the very essence of the psychoanalytic method. What can one ever reply to the complaint, "Why didn't you say that before?" One's new idea is already old by the time it can be voiced. There is nothing to be ashamed of in this; it is the only correct, the only effectual position to be in. The method demands it. My allegiance to the method had never faltered. One must have faith in the method and follow its dictates. Was there here any room for doubt?

The claret began to pulse through my veins. I mean *that* wine, Keats's old wine of heaven, the redigestion of our most ethereal musings on earth. Hamlet was gone, for ever. In his absence I had only his story to scrutinize, only my own company in which to digest it. Jesting Pilate could not wait for his answer, but after eight years perhaps the truth was in fact waiting for me, enfolded within Hamlet's story – that journey of re-membering which I was about to begin. Already in formulating my quest I could glimpse the possibility of a different pain at the end of it, the joyful pain of understanding.

> So let me speak to th' yet unknowing world
> How these things came about!

July 1973. Hamlet Dane, the only child of wealthy middle class parents, was referred to me shortly after his nineteenth birthday for being "impossible" at home: "insufferably rude" and aggressive in his behaviour. *The transformation of both the interior and the exterior man.* His disturbance manifest itself at times in states of extreme withdrawal, during which he would spend hours scribbling in his diary at night, and most of the day asleep, ignoring everybody else in the house. At other times it took the form of wild outbursts of shouting, pushing furniture about and so on. One night he had bolted his parents out of the house and they had had to call the police. All this took place when he returned home for the long vacation after his first year reading English at Cambridge University.

I had had some acquaintance with Hamlet's parents before meeting them to discuss his case. His mother, a gracious and elegant woman of French birth, with liquid dark eyes, was well known for her excellent cuisine and dinner parties, frequented by all the Hampstead intelligentsia. She had a reputation for taking a keen interest in young artists and writers, presiding in effect over a type of literary *salon*. His father was an industrialist, impressive of stature, with gentle green eyes and a wide, sensual, melancholy mouth. He looked, I thought, tired and slightly stooping when I met him this time, while his wife seemed more beautiful than I had remembered. Their worry about Hamlet was exacerbated, they explained, by their total incomprehension. For though they were well aware of adolescent rebellions, negativism and even breakdowns, there seemed no reason for any of this in Hamlet's case. It was as though he had become an alien being. His hostility seemed particularly directed against his father, to whom as a young child he had been very attached.

"Every time he passes Claude on the stairs or wherever (he doesn't eat with us any more, you see)", explained his mother, "he says 'howdy uncle', or jerks his fingers in some obscene gesture. He really means it, it's most upsetting. After he'd been behaving like this for a while, I told him we'd had enough of his infantile tasteless jokes. Then he gave me such a look, I can't describe it – wild, vicious, almost actual hatred. *Such black and grained spots he saw in my soul.* It was horrible."

While she spoke, Claude winced visibly. Then she added: "And for some time now he's been insulting his father, accusing him of drinking too much – sometimes even in public, either openly or through innuendo. Which is nonsense – Claude drinks socially, like everyone else." *A custom more honour'd in the breach than the observance.*

"We do seem to have more social obligations than many people", Claude put in wryly.

"No more than could be helped, with your position and commitments", said his wife to him a little defensively, then, turning to me, she explained that in fact they were trying to cut down on their social engagements, since Claude had had a minor stroke the previous winter. I asked if this had appeared to worry Hamlet.

"Rather the opposite", said his father; "he seems to have taken it as a cue to add to *our* worries." Then he proceeded to explain his own position as a parent: how he was not a domineering father, and Hamlet had never been forced to do anything against his will, nor had unreasonable demands been made of him.

"You must understand, Dr Horacio", he said, *more in sorrow than in anger* or resentment, "we are not the sort of grossly ambitious parents who would drive their son in some direction that was unsuitable for him. There's no reason for him to turn against us."

"That is very true", confirmed his wife. "All we want is for him to fulfil his own interests in life. We would be perfectly happy if he wanted to become a writer, for example." *A soldier, scholar, statesman.*

"I know what it is to suffer from parental pressures", continued Claude. "It's true that at one time I did hope he'd eventually succeed me in the business. But when it became clear that that was not for him, I never tried to force him into it. I was disappointed of course. He's a clever boy, we realize that – his teachers have always had great expectations of him. The professor at Cambridge tells us he's one of the most promising students he's ever had."

What about girlfriends? I queried. His mother looked animated: "Now I did suspect it might have something to do with a girlfriend", she said, "not that Hamlet has ever actually brought a girl home as yet. I thought his diary might give me a clue – he's been writing avidly in it ever since he came home. *Setting in his tables how one may smile and smile and be a villain.* But these days he keeps it locked. Besides, I thought, this is ridiculous. He's too old to have his secrets prized out that way – what good would it do? No, I thought, if he can't confide in me straightforwardly, then it's better we find him someone else to talk to." *Thou art a scholar, Horatio – speak to him.*

Claude nodded. "Gertrude thinks he needs to let it all out – you know – in front of somebody other than just the two of us." Then he added, rather furtively, "Do you suppose there's anything you can do about him – I mean, for him?"

I said that I hoped so. Hamlet's symptoms verged on the extreme but that was not uncharacteristic of adolescence. I noted the indications of incipient violence and the "Howdy uncle" business but thought best not to draw too much attention to these at that point.

"A type of *normal* madness, you mean?" suggested Claude, "that requires an adjustment of everyone's values, relatively speaking? That's what I used to tell my own father!"

Possibly, I agreed, it could be the degree rather than the kind which exceeded the bounds of the "normal". *A madness north-north-west.* It was hard to say until I had met him, and seen how he took to working with the psychoanalytic method. Extracting my diary, I said I could offer him three sessions a week from September. His parents looked rather astonished. I apologized for only being able to offer three sessions, but pointed out that Hamlet would find it difficult to come down from Cambridge during the term for more than that (he could come, say, on a weekday evening, a Saturday and a Monday morning), and in any case it was always difficult to get adolescents for more than two or three sessions a week.

"Oh dear – we'd hoped you might be able to discover what was wrong with him before he went back", confessed his mother. *The very cause of Hamlet's lunacy.* Now it was my turn to feel a little stunned. Whatever the nature of his problem, I said, it was bound to involve more than mere diagnosis. Gertrude smiled apologetically, and said, "You're quite right, Dr Horacio – we're too impatient. Psychoanalysis isn't an instant cure. That's why it works, isn't it?"

Unfortunately, I had to say, there was never any guarantee of a cure. The very concept of "cure" was no longer considered as valid as it had seemed in the past. But adolescence was always a turbulent and dynamic period, and I was hopeful. Claude asked if they would receive regular progress reports, and I explained it was not usually appropriate. It was detrimental to the analytic relationship for the adolescent to sense too much conferring behind the scenes; the analyst had to be experienced as an independent figure.

"I see", Claude laughed ruefully; "all I need to do now is pay the monthly bill." He was clearly relieved that somebody else was prepared to take his son's disturbance seriously. Gertrude frowned disapprovingly at him, and said she had one more worry: Hamlet was planning to go on a long trekking holiday to India that summer – was he in a fit state of responsibility? This news did rather worry me, and I asked whether he had manifest any behavioural problems outside his home – at college, for example?

"None that we know of", said his father; "and we know his tutor very well. I'm sure he'd have told us if he'd noticed anything. All he ever says is how delighted he is with Hamlet's progress, in fact with everything about Hamlet." With mournful irony he added, "Hamlet is the apple of his eye."

In that case, I replied (somewhat helplessly), it would probably be reasonable for him to go; I imagined it would be impossible to stop him anyway – was he going alone?

"No", said Gertrude, "he's going with a friend, someone we've known for ages – the son of his tutor, Professor Polack, in fact. He's a bit older than Hamlet, and he's been before. I wouldn't necessarily call him more responsible, though, in the normal way of things."

"They'll be all right", said Claude decisively. "It will do him good." I sensed his relief at having his son off their home territory for a while. *Author of his own remove.*

After the Danes had left, I meditated on the strong appeal of their personal qualities, their modesty and openness. This was the first private conversation I had had with either of them, though I too had been to their parties and been impressed by the glittering ambience of highly tasteful, cultured wealth and manners. Undoubtedly I was younger than many of the psychoanalysts with whom they had contact; but instinctively, I felt, they had chosen someone eager to respond to the challenge of their troublesome son. It was an interesting fact, I reflected (not for the first time) that even children of the most sensitive and devoted parents, brought up in conditions of privilege, were still not immune to psychological disturbance.

I had one preliminary interview with Hamlet himself before the summer holiday. He was one of those teenagers who is clearly unhappy on their feet: he arrived at my house in Flask Walk on a bike, which he leant unlocked against the railings just outside the semi-basement window of my consulting room. He loped down the steps and rang. As he was just on time for his appointment, I admitted him directly and he sat down on the chair in the corner of the room, whence he could scan simultaneously the bike, the couch and myself. I was struck by his resemblance to his mother – an angular and lanky version of her poised and graceful figure, with identical dark eyes, though his were half hidden by long and greasy locks of hair. For a couple of minutes he darted an occasional hawk-like glance at me from behind his hair.

"I expect you'll say you can't psychoanalyse me unless I lie on the couch", he commenced. "Well I'm afraid I'm not going to, because to my mind, nothing could be more ridiculous."

I explained that this was simply an introductory meeting, and there was no hurry to use the couch until he felt ready to do so. The function of the couch was to help him collect his thoughts and associations, free from the distraction of looking at me, the analyst. I gave my usual explanation of my way of working with the psychoanalytic method: the discipline of the routine, the setting, the fifty-minute sessions, etc.; the importance of trying to be frank in relating whatever came into his mind during the session, however absurd it might seem, rather than storing up things to tell me outside the sessions; above all, the importance of trying to remember his dreams. At this last, a wave of panic clouded his eyes beneath the hair, and he assured me he didn't dream, and certainly couldn't remember his dreams. "And as for telling you all the things that might cross my mind while I'm sitting here, I can't imagine anything more boring. It'd be like trying to write an essay without giving it a moment's thought – just scribbling one word after another."

In practice, I said, he would find that only things relevant to the analytic situation – that is, the emotional situation – would come to his mind. That was the beauty of the method. All I required was for him to relate them honestly to me.

He parted a strand of hair over one eye and peered intensely at me: "You really are weird", he said. "What a peculiar idea – to call a method beautiful – even if it is a method, and I don't see that it is a method at all. Not a scientific method."

I commented that inevitably, this was something he would come to understand only with experience. He seemed a little stung by this minor rebuke, and said condescendingly:

"You'll find I know a lot more about this business than my uncle does. He's never given it a thought till he got it into his head to send me here. He's desperate to get rid of me, you see. As a matter of fact", he added provocatively, "I *put* it into his head. I'm interested in expanding my mind." *Thoughts beyond the reaches of our souls.*

He paused, eyeing me for effect. Why his "uncle"? I asked.

"Uncle Claude, of course", he said in a matter-of-fact tone, but with a defiant, piercing stare. "You've met him, haven't you?" *My uncle-father.*

"Ah", I said, and then asked Hamlet what he had found out about psychoanalysis.

"Well", he began to chatter, "To start with, I've read quite a bit – introductions to the various schools and all that – I got a reading list from my director of studies, he's surprisingly into it. That's just background of course. Then I've got a couple of friends who've actually been psychoanalysed. Rosenfeld's still having his complexes sorted out – he had a terrible childhood, his parents just dumped him at school and went globetrotting.

He used to come into the prefects' common room at lunchtime, after his session, and tell us what else they'd discovered about what his parents had done to his primary processes before his memory became conscious. He was having a Freudian analysis, but Gildstein – the other guy – had a Kleinian one, so I got the chance to compare the two. Gildstein's mother actually is a psychoanalyst, so he had it prophylactically when he was quite young, to stop him getting anything later. The Kleinians believe in prevention rather than cure, don't they – aren't you a Kleinian?" *Rosencrantz and gentle Guildenstern.*

Under cover of his naivety (and I couldn't quite make out whether this was genuine or assumed), he was giving the impression of a cat waiting to pounce. I realized I would have to be on my guard with this Elephant's Child. I pointed out that his friends' stories still came into the category of hearsay (or "background" as he called it) and he should be prepared to find his own experience rather different. But, since he had clearly made some inquiries about my background, I asked him what other information he had discovered about me? *In questionable shape.*

"You're a great writer of scientific papers, aren't you", he replied immediately. I quailed, on my guard. When I asked if he had read any, he replied "Well sort of. Can't say I was impressed by your style – too much jargon. And some of your ideas are a bit oldfashioned. But yeah – it was OK" (he said, drumming his fingers on his knee). "But I'm surprised the people you're writing about let you get away with it – exposing all their secrets in public like that." *Hunting the trail of policy.*

I saw he was convinced that I would want to write a "scientific paper" about him, and also nervous about my doing so. I explained that such papers were written for other clinical practitioners and had a very limited circulation and intelligibility, and that the identity of patients was protected by altering names and other features.

"Names! What's in a *name*?" he exclaimed contemptuously, as if I were either very casual or very credulous. "You wouldn't be able to write anything about me, with my parentage, without everybody knowing exactly who you were talking about. 'Oh yes now, the Dane boy', they'll be gossiping behind their whisky glasses, 'he's been seeing Dr Horacio lately; now you know what his problem turns out to be ...' blah blah blah."

I caught an early glimpse here of the grandiosity, in its attention-seeking context, which was to prove a central problem in the analysis; and already it worried me. To defuse it, I explained to Hamlet that there was also a more subtle form of protection, founded on the nature of the psychoanalytic relationship and the countertransference of the analyst's reception of the patient's feelings, which meant that it was understood the analyst was always writing subjectively – and in essence, about himself. He grinned as he took this in.

"Oh very good", he said. "I like it – real slippery, man. So nobody gets to find out the real secret after all." *The centre where truth is hid.*

It was rather, I said, that the concept of their being "a secret" was a mistaken one. It was better to think of the mind as "having mystery" than as "hiding secrets".

"Oh yeah?" he taunted suspiciously. "You're not religious or anything, are you?"

The psychoanalytic method, I told him, was designed to focus on mental events – thoughts, feelings, the organization and interaction of internal figures or objects. These were difficult to observe and understand, which was why we relied so much on dreams to "tell the truth" about an internal situation.

"I don't see how psychoanalysis can cure if it can't even find out what's wrong", he said, "whether you call it a secret or a mystery."

I agreed that our goal was better defined as observing, clarifying, understanding, than curing. He meditated on this for a moment and then concluded that that, of course, was exactly why he had come – not to be cured (it was not as though there were anything wrong with him) but to investigate his inner mystery. *The heart of the mystery.*

On his way out he noticed that I held out my hand and he gave it a hurried and embarrassed shake. This initial meeting made an enduring impression on me. I was touched by his eagerness to investigate himself, and by his willingness to almost immediately view me as someone to whom he could attach a childlike dependence. He had been ready, almost before seeing me, to adopt me as the real friend whom he evidently felt he lacked. It was clear that he had motivated his parents to seek out an analyst for him. But I was worried, also, by a certain fixedness in his attitude: he had a preformed idea of my function as an analyst and how I would serve him; and, above all, it seemed clear that the confusion about his "uncle-father" had the fixed structure of a delusion, with its attendant danger of incipient schizophrenia.

For his first analytic session, some two months later, Hamlet arrived on his bike as before and entered the consulting room with a busy, eager air, wearing a long blue Indian shirt, patched jeans and sandals. He had a newly grown beard. He glanced around and nodded at me, as though my presence in the room were a fortuitous event – one more accident befalling him on his travels. Then, rather to my surprise, he flung himself down on the couch and began to talk animatedly, moving his arms, about the people and events which had filled his summer holidays. He had gone to India with a friend named Nando ("short for Ferdinand – his father's Italian"), and the account of their travels (which I realized I was not the first to listen to) was clearly embellished and glamourized with each successive telling, though it included spending a week prostrate with severe diarrhoea, and on the way home, two nights in a Turkish jail under suspicion of drugs trafficking. *Thieves of mercy.* This last was recounted as if it were the highlight of a royal tour from which his return was eagerly awaited. *Hamlet the Dane.*

"Rosenfeld and Gildstein are back too", he announced meaningfully, turning his head from the couch as though to clinch his demonstration that his entire court now surrounded him. (Needless to say I had only the haziest recollection of who Rosenfeld and Gildstein might be.) *Guildenstern and gentle Rosencrantz.*

The air of prickly awkwardness which had characterized Hamlet on our original meeting had vanished. But there was no sign, either, of the few moments of emotional contact. I gathered I was supposed to be impressed by his new man-of-the-world bearing; and I was pondering on this, he broke off his narration and accused me of not listening:

"I suppose you're really only interested in my sex life", he said provocatively.

I replied that I would like to hear more about his friend Nando – had he known him long?

"For ever", he yawned. "He was rugby captain at school – the year above me. Yeah, he's a great one for boasting about his sexual exploits – you guessed. Nando's all right though. It was OK going away with him, you knew he wouldn't leave you in the lurch" (this was the first indication there could have been any "lurches"). "He's very into transcendental meditation and the alternative society. He's left home of course and now he shares a house with some friends in Islington. His dad's my supervisor at Cambridge – though you'd never believe Nando was sired by an intellectual wizard."

The intellectual wizard, Professor Polack, was to figure prominently in the analysis, as would all the members of the Polack family. His schoolboy homosexual relationship with Nando was soon to transfer to an intense involvement with his sister Ophelia. I learned that Hamlet had in fact known the family since childhood, and until recently had been at school with Nando, who had stayed on as a boarder when his father and sister moved to Cambridge. From his first year as a student Hamlet had been filled with an intense admiration for the Professor, and as far as I could gather, this seemed to be more or less reciprocated. Meanwhile I was told the "amazing" history of Polack's arrival in England. An Italian Jew whose father had been "something high up in politics" before the war, his original name was Polaco. When the war came all his family were killed in concentration camps, and he only survived because an English girl helped him to escape – via ox-carts, guards'-vans, and the bilge of a fishing boat – until she got him to England and married him. She died when the children were very young, and the Professor brought them up on his own – according to Hamlet, heroically concentrating on their education:

"It cost him a fortune to keep Nando at school, you know. As for Ophelia, he had her made into a fabulous musician – she can play anything from the cello to a host of weird medieval instruments. Come to think of it", he added, "they've both had far more attention showered on them than my parents ever paid me."

Here was a surprising departure, I thought – hadn't he been given opportunities by his parents which were at least the equivalent of the Polack children's?

"Conventionally speaking, maybe", he acquiesced rather pompously. "But not in real terms. I was just supposed to fit the bill – come top in exams, bow and scrape to the guests at home, make polite conversation – do my stuff however screwed up I felt inside. The performing dog." *Subject to my birth.* Then he explained, confidentially, "I expect the early death of his wife helped. That meant he could bring Nando and Ophelia up the way he wanted – no interference."

It was interesting, I commented ironically, that a feature of Hamlet's grievance was that he had two parents instead of one – implying that mothers were not really necessary, just background. He spoke as though his two parents, being conjoined in some confusing way, had somehow prevented his being "thought about" such that he could develop upwards in a clean straight line, as Ophelia had grown straight up into a musician. By contrast he, Hamlet, felt he was growing "screwed up". *Out of joint.*

At this he turned on me with a sudden vehemence, and said, "OK, so I've been lumbered with a whole load of inherited problems. My uncle for a start. Anyone can see what a debauched, drunken, degenerate old lecher he is – yet my mother thinks the sun shines out of his arse. But I could tolerate that if it wasn't for the hypocrisy and vanity of them all. The trouble with adults is, they can't understand the difference between training and education. *The creatures that are mine.* They want their children to perform well in their circus – and for whose sake? Certainly not the children's. Look at me – I haven't been brought up, I've been *bred* – like a horse on a prize stud farm – groomed in everything from table manners to socialist politics. And it's all for their own vanity and self-satisfaction – at best – and at worst it's so they can show off to their court at the next dinner party!"

I was taken aback and rather stung by this outburst. Clearly Hamlet was accusing me of being one of the adult trainers who merely wished to bring him into line for their egotistical satisfaction. I remembered the time when I had made a similar distinction about training and education to my own father, although – I believe – in a less hurtful manner (I never really quarrelled with him). I told Hamlet he was complaining about institutional values – the stud farm – as a way of ignoring the more complex problems associated with intimate relationships, such as with his parents. In rejecting these as institutional, so beneath his notice, he was avoiding their real difficulties.

"It's they who think we're beneath *their* notice", retorted Hamlet. "The standard adult line is that children can be seen and heard, but only saying the right things. And they're quite oblivious to the fact that the children might be seeing and hearing *them*. No – *they're* the ones who are always playing at secrets; they're the ones who can't tell the difference between a secret and a mystery!"

He was an interesting boy, I thought, after this little altercation. There was more perspicacity in his criticism of the adult world than in the standard adolescent defiance, and at the same time more delusion. His mother was seen to be tainted by her adhesiveness to his contemptible uncle-father, who had himself been split off from his real father. Presumably he had ensconced himself in the Professor's affections as an alternative to this. I began to form a picture of the seriously entrenched nature of Hamlet's grandiosity – his overpowering need to show off and be admired, to be indeed the prize horse in the stud. Thus, one session, he was full of how he had just been to dinner at Polack's house, along with some other students, and been the life and soul of the party owing to his satirical impersonations of public figures, which had delighted the Professor. This was recounted in the midst of other social triumphs: the engineering of crushing blows against the establishment, such as getting the college authorities to install a condom machine in the toilet and a photocopying machine for the Junior Common Room, on the grounds of equality of dissemination of information.

The session after this, he brought me an interesting little dream which illuminated the tongue-in-cheek nature of his idealized view of the Polack family relationships. *The dream began with a birds'-eye view of glittering blue ocean, in the midst of which was a small speck. Gradually this came into nearer focus (as in a film) and showed itself to be a tiny picture-postcard island with a ring of yellow sand, and coconut palms. In the middle of the ring stood Professor Polack, dressed like a children's magician in a huge purple cloak spangled with stars and moons, his arms upraised with a wand in one hand and his bald head with its pointed beard looking upwards to the sky.*

"I realized he was saying something, as if he was casting a spell. He seemed to be saying, "Grow, my children; grow, and prosper!" Then I could see there was a big white cloud above his head, soft and puffy against the blue sky, like those rococo ceilings, those cloud-capped towers. And Nando and Ophelia were sitting cross-legged in the centre of the cloud, dressed in gold and white kaftans, with a chess board between them, but instead of moving chessmen they were putting chocolates in each other's mouths."

Hamlet seemed amused by this dream, saying it was like a mixture of chocolate and insurance adverts. "It's a classic wish-fulfilment dream", he pronounced. "Wish-fulfilment for adults, that is. They set up some scenario exactly like an advert and put the children in the middle to act out their fantasies for them. Now children – grow up nicely, and be a credit to your doting parents. What good children, taking their exams and eating their chocolates! 'Prosper' – that's a pun on status-making of course. Aristocratic pretensions, all of them."

Yes, I agreed, this dream showed us his underlying mockery of the Professor's methods of upbringing, in which the entire adult world was implicated, with some justification. In Hamlet's view, the Professor with his wand thinks he is "raising" the children, handing down wisdom – ignorant that secretly (including through sexual games) the children are really raising themselves.

But as well as Hamlet's mockery of the Professor's self-idealization and the complicity of brother and sister in it, the dream also suggested his essential loneliness as an only child who had no-one in the family with whom to share his childishness – only adults.

Hamlet then told me of a strange vision, or memory-flash, he had had the other day when sitting with Nando and his friends doing transcendental meditation "for a laugh". An image of Ophelia from some years before had come vividly to his mind. In this, she was sitting perched on her brother's shoulders during a political demonstration; it was one of the few occasions he had seen her in London since she had moved to Cambridge.

"She was wearing a green duffle coat with her long fair hair falling right down over his face. Her mouth was very pink, it kept opening and shutting, and the air was grey and frosty. Her breath was rising up in clouds. Lucy in the sky with diamonds. She was chanting rhythmically, 'pigs go home'. She looked really angry, kind of transported."

I asked Hamlet if the Polack brother and sister were particularly good-looking, to which he assented rather casually, sounding surprised, adding that Nando had sometimes been nicknamed Adonis at school. "But she's more talented than he is", he corrected me, lest I should imagine he was swayed by such superficial characteristics as physical beauty. God gave one face, why make themselves another. Ophelia's face on Nando's shoulders, I suggested, implied that Nando had the body and Ophelia the brains of their brother-sister combination; it was she who held the reins.

"Nando's not stupid", said Hamlet, "he's just not academic."

Nevertheless I suspected that Hamlet's hero-worship of the rugger-captain Adonis-Nando had a rather tentative quality, as did his idealization of his magician father. I also noted there was something a little unsavoury about the sister, with her "pigs go home" – who were the pigs?

"I dunno", said Hamlet nonchalantly, "police I suppose – can't remember."

This was in a sense the underside to the chocolate picture – showing how the children had the upper hand, were the driving force of the adult world, under the guise of jigging and lisping and nicknaming God's creatures. Again, there seemed to be something of Hamlet's own infancy in it. Thinking of Hamlet's solitary childhood, I asked him if there might be any connection with riding on his father's shoulders when he was very young. He agreed with surprise that he could remember doing that. *Borne on his back a thousand times, and now how abhorred in his imagination.* And I described to him the glimpse I now had of the boy-Hamlet, elevated by his father's stature yet believing that he had elevated himself and was in fact the only real king, directing and controlling his father's movements. *Make your lady laugh.*

We parted after this session with a mutual wary interest. I had a much clearer idea of the seriousness of his problem – his grandiosity, with its infantile roots in his relationship with his father, and the delusional form it had now taken with the despised "uncle-father" who was no longer responsive to his direction and to the mutual idealization he demanded. At the same time I was impressed, and surprised, by his co-operativeness and eagerness – different from the usual aggression and antagonism of the adolescent. I was stirred by both his incisiveness and his dependence. For underneath his contempt for the follies of the adult world, I could sense strongly the lonely child's nostalgia for being Daddy's boy. Perhaps this spoke to me more readily as I had no son, and felt this a gap in my life. Already I could foresee a pattern of transference relationships forming in which I knew I should have to tread carefully. In the intensity of Hamlet's desire to explore his mystery and to be admired, something he had attached to Polack – and previously to his father – was already beginning to transfer itself to me. *Speak to it, Horatio.*

CHAPTER TWO

The Ghost

Ghost: If thou has nature in thee, bear it not,
   Let not the royal bed of Denmark be
   A couch for luxury and damned incest.
   But howsomever thou pursuest this act,
   Taint not thy mind, nor let thy soul contrive
   Against thy mother aught. (I. v. 82-86)

Horacio is surprised by the sudden impact of Ophelia after Hamlet's dream of the Ghost, and begins to tackle Hamlet's ambivalence towards women.

The week after this, Hamlet brought me a fascinating and crucial dream, whose mirroring of deep emotional conflicts would prove central to the analysis for a long time. The Ghost dream became a major point of reference for us.

In this dream, *Hamlet saw his father in his fighter-pilot's uniform from the war, seated inside his Spitfire wearing flying suit and goggles. He seemed larger than life, surrounded by a shimmering golden aura, and the plane's wings seemed to be quivering in a violent wind. Their shadow enveloped Hamlet as he stood outside the plane and shivered. Hamlet felt tiny by contrast with his father in the plane, and intimidated. Above all, he felt bewildered and wanted desperately to know what was happening, and he cried out:*

> "Let me not burst in ignorance! Why do you
> Shake my nature with such awesome thoughts
> Beyond the utmost reaching of my soul?
> Say why! What should I think? What must I do?"

At this point his father raised his goggles to reveal his face, and moved his lips in reply, though his voice itself was inaudible and its sound seemed to be transferred through the beating of the plane's wings. In this way, Hamlet heard his father's complaint about his own unhappiness and its history:

> "O Hamlet! The secrets of my prison-house
> Are the fruits of lust, your mother's lust,
> That seeming-virtuous angel whose sweet milk
> Turned all to sourness and to sadness – a drink
> Most serpentine – the day she treacherously
> Abandoned me by weaning as I lay
> On Lethe's wharf, and rooted at my ease.
> Placidly rocking and unsuspecting, I was
> Ignorant that her desires had turned
> Elsewhere."

Hamlet noticed that his father was turning to start the plane for takeoff. So again he asked urgently what he should "do", and his father said in the same ghostly tones, transmitted through vibrations in the wind,

> "Remember me, my son! And seek revenge.
> But however you choose to set about it,
> Taint not your mind nor harm your mother."

Then the noise of the engine drowned all other sounds as the plane began to move down the runway. But first it circled Hamlet three times, and he noticed painted on the plane's nose the seductive image of a girl in bathing costume, and the name in twirly lettering, "Gertrude".

I was thrilled with the imaginative richness of this dream, with its direct – if ambiguous – focusing on Hamlet's troubled relationship with his father, and having his mother as a key gravitational force in the background, both attracting and repelling. The dream certainly had a glamorous quality, which Hamlet associated with his father's decorations for bravery that hung in the lobby of their home, including photographs of his parents' wedding and of his father standing by his plane in wartime. In this sense the dream showed his father-as-hero, protecting his mother or mother country from invasion in the war. *He smote the sledded Polacks on the ice.* At the same time it showed him his aggressiveness towards women – relating this to the infant at weaning, feeling abandoned by this wife/mother at the same time as becoming conscious of his dependence on her.

This father, whose ambiguity stemmed from his ambiguous internal picture of womanhood, seemed to transfer his own quandary to Hamlet in the dream. Hamlet himself was excluded from the dizzy sexual heights (and dangers) attained by the plane (with his mother's name); his father was taking off without him. But, I wondered, mulling over his father's final words, in what precise sense was the model of sexuality he presented one of "revenge"?

"It's revenge on my mother for taking up with Uncle Claude, of course", pronounced Hamlet, who had been listening to my ruminations with an air of bemused impatience. "There's something shameful, at her age, about the way she fusses and fawns all over him – even more since he's been ill. It's degraded, when you consider what my father was like – but she's only got herself to blame."

I asked him to explain to me the difference between his "father" and "Uncle Claude". *Hyperion and the satyr.* He responded eagerly, as though at last he'd been given the opportunity to set this straight:

"Things were quite different before Uncle Claude took over. Everybody admired my father – he was generous, idealistic, strong. There was nothing sneaky or underhand about him, everything was open and above board. He was the kind of man who, if he had lived, would really have made a difference to society – because he meant what he said, and he would have carried it out. Not like Claude ..." (and here he began to list scornfully the evidence, in his eyes, of his father's physical and mental decay – his illness, drinking too heavily, problems of finance and industrial relations at the major chemical factory which he had established, owned and directed). "And now he is being investigated by the Inland Revenue. So much for being a respectable capitalist with socialist principles! I suppose he thought he could get away for ever with having it both ways. It just shows – if he's not screwing a woman he's screwing the workers. Yuck. Degeneration in mind and body." *Th'impostume of much wealth and peace.*

I saw that in Hamlet's mind his father literally seemed to have become someone else – though still a close relative, the "brother" of his former self. The wartime captain of nobility and heroism, and genuine socialist beliefs, had been exchanged for the usurping industrial chief. *Unhousel'd, disappointed, unaneal'd.* I asked him at what point this transformation seemed to have taken place, and he said he couldn't remember precisely because he must have been quite young, but he remembered vividly when the truth of what had happened first began to dawn upon him, when he was thirteen or fourteen. At that time he began to think for himself – his eyes were opened, and he regretted having gone along with his mother in pretending that there was nothing wrong, because then it became crystal clear to him what a mess this weak hypocritical ploy had made of their family relationships.

"That's what's so pathetic about the older generation", said Hamlet in a bitterly scathing tone; "they think they're so clever at hiding secrets from the new generation, even when it's blatantly obvious to everyone what's going on."

I said it was Hamlet's conviction that his mother, well-intentioned but foolish, had kept his father's death when he was a young child a secret from him, hoping that he wouldn't remember and that Claude would be a completely satisfactory stepfather for him. Without making any direct reply to this interpretation, he continued vigorously as though more evidence was required to convince me of his mother's folly.

"The end result is, it's *me* who has to tell her what she's doing wrong – because it's only herself she manages to blind. You see, Dr Horacio, my mother thought she could cover it all over by holding court in her drawing room, surrounded by sycophants and flatterers – the best class of people, of course, with impeccable views on politics and cultures – all enviously grateful for being allowed to participate in such scintillating conversation and to swill booze with Claude from the cellar that never runs dry. Life with the Danes – pillars of society and civilization on the surface, and a rotting dungheap of social climbers underneath!" *Something is rotten in the state of Denmark.*

Returning to the dream, whose rich cellar of imagery I felt we had only begun to tap, I showed him how the image of the father-as-hero now demanded adjustment in the light of his own adolescent turbulence, including his jaundiced view of the adult world now that his "eyes were opened".

"All that aeroplane stuff, of course", said Hamlet dismissively, "belongs to when I was a little boy and was mad about planes and wanted to be a pilot myself. That makes this dream outdated. A Ghost-pilot from the past."

The dream, however, was about now, not about then. The hero-father who had returned like a ghost from the past history of his boyhood ideals now seemed to be introducing him to the anxieties of adulthood. These were looming over him like the wings of his father's aeroplane. In particular, he was being introduced to his own ambivalence towards women, by a father whose role seemed to be that of both protector and conqueror. *Taint not your mind.* This upsurgence within himself was what was now troubling him. *So horridly shaking his disposition.*

"It seems to me that *they're* the ones who are in trouble", said Hamlet with a casual disdain, ignoring my interpretation of his personal conflict. "They should have a health warning written all over them – 'Avoid my example – I'm obsolete'. They just can't adjust to the way things are now. In the war it was all right and wrong, good and bad. United goals and jolly camaraderie – with God on their side. That was easy. Now they've lost their sense of direction and it's all wheeling and dealing, shuffling and committee meetings. Bribery and corruption. Drink and debauchery."

Hamlet's persistent and perspicacious variation on the usual adolescent theme of how the children had long discovered everything the adults had tried to hide from them, was that the adults themselves were really children without knowing it. Nevertheless I wanted to remind him of his own personal helplessness, which had been clearly expressed in the dream. *He could be bounded in a nutshell were it not that he had bad dreams.*

"Yeah, maybe", he drawled, more aggressively, "but the fact is it's us lot – the new generation – who are going to be lumbered with sorting *them* out."

The dream, I stressed, showed that the first place he needed to look to begin to "sort things out" was inside himself, at his own internal condition. Instead of attributing blame to his internal father-and-mother, he needed to locate the positive qualities they could offer to help him work through his own conflicts.

"Internal father and mother! They look a pretty insalubrious pair to me", he mocked. *Uncle-father and aunt-mother.* "More like Status and Self-gratification – that's their scene in a nutshell."

Status and self-gratification, I agreed, could certainly be defined as unhelpful qualities, which could take "revenge" on him and distort his mental growth. Our job in the analysis was to disentangle these from the genuinely parental qualities to be found in his internal objects.

"Oh yeah – disentangle – I like it!" he sneered. "The fact is, when you get right down to it – no one wants a feller with a social disease. *Our mothers all are junkies, our fathers all are punks …*"

He concluded, addressing me slyly as he left, "OK, Officer Krupke?"

I pondered, after he had gone, on his quick switches of attitude to me and these other parental figures. At one moment he would cooperate with me, as much in the sense of conspiring as of being helped (with a definite element of showing-off); the next moment, I was relegated to being some constricting authority figure. My technique with him was not made easier by his innate deftness at twisting our conversation into the form of a debate – a form with which he obviously felt familiar and in control, and where winning his point took precedence over confronting the truth about himself. He had a natural talent for avoiding the intimate emotionality with which my interpretations tried to bring him in touch. And yet, it was all there in his dream. Once again, I admired its richness. The Ghost dream was to be the first in a series of imaginative dreams that astounded me by their emotional depth and awareness, each time inspiring me with new hope even when in utter despondency.

It was, however, a strange phenomenon – that despite his perspicacity, even brilliance, Hamlet did not seem to have grasped the concept of learning from an individual, or of being taught by them. His immediate attachment to me – from our first meeting – had an automatic quality, not a reciprocal quality founded on real appreciation and the growth of trust in me. *His soul sealed me for itself.* This made me think of the Professor, who, I suspected, now filled the gap left by Hamlet's early idealization of his father. And in turn, I was reminded of certain troubling factors in my own life: anxiety about the prospect of my daughters' adolescence; the vague sense that my wife and I had drifted apart; above all, regret that I had no son. My countertransference involvement with Hamlet made me acutely conscious of all these factors, especially the last. Had I, perhaps, idealized Hamlet's parents, leaping to conclusions about their excellence, as a way of escaping my own anxieties and problems in this difficult and unsatisfactory sphere? Was there more truth in his criticism of them than I had cared to investigate? I worried as I did recurrently with other patients, whether I tended to get too involved with my analytic work, investing too much personal emotion in it at the expense of my home life.

Meanwhile, over the next few days, my reflections returned to Hamlet's relationship with his new substitute-father, the Professor, and I wondered how it would progress. I was curious to observe its evolution. But before I heard more about this, Hamlet's sudden intimacy with the Professor's daughter burst in on the analysis, taking me by surprise with its intensity and rapidity, although I was aware of her existence in the background.

One evening, Hamlet came in curiously garbed, with a profusion of chains and bangles worn over his leather jacket with its collar up, and dark glasses propped above his forehead (he had by now shaved his beard). *His nighted colour.* I was struck immediately by a resemblance to the Ghost-pilot of his dream and remarked that his armoury gave him an inaccessible appearance. He countered sharply:

"It isn't me that's inaccessible. It's that frigid tart. She is avoiding me – not entirely (that would at least be honest), but she won't even come out with me alone any more. So I see her every day, but always surrounded by a bodyguard of friends, or her father. Or else she's 'got to work'."

Who is this? I interrupted – Polack's daughter?

"Yes, Ophelia!" he snapped irritably. "Last night, if you want to know, I dreamed *I flew into her window – a sort of Batman act, storming the citadel – and had her.*

> *Loosed out of hell to speak of horrors,*
> *I came before her,*
> *Heaving a sigh so piteous and profound*
> *It seemed to shatter all my bulk*
> *And end my being.*

I realized of course that was just how she wanted it – that's what would fulfil her typical feminine fantasies – swept up like the princess in the tower, all virginal and starry-eyed. And that, of course", he added with a savage cynicism, "is their prescription for how it's got to *seem* to be, whatever the dirty realities might be underneath it all. *Is or seems* – they don't know the difference."

Hamlet then explained, in response to my query, that Ophelia did not live at home with her father, though she was often there at weekends, but had a room at her women's college – an "institution like a nunnery" – and her window was on the second floor, as in the dream. However, he had no intention of shinning up a drainpipe like Romeo: "The hypocrisy of the whole affair – that's what's so disgusting. I don't mean only her, but everybody. No men are allowed in there after 11 at night, which simply means there's a man stowed in every cupboard. *Safely stowed.* And I'm only interested in equal sex, not some archaic fantasy of wooing and conquering. What's the point of pretending to worship virginity these days? It's Edwardian – yet we still haven't caught up with Shaw's diagnosis. Marriage contracts and all that paraphernalia are simply designed to perpetuate social hierarchies. We haven't learned to separate the social disguise from the itch in the flesh which should be honestly viewed for what it is. *The lewdness that will sate itself.* It's time the cobwebs were swept away and some clear thinking was introduced."

It was the first time I had seen Hamlet in the full flow of a rant, though it was not to be the last. It was a curious phenomenon – unleashed, as I took it, by the Ghost within him. *Loosed out of hell.*

"It's all pretence anyway", he added with renewed vehemence. "When you get right down to it – behind all the simpering and fluttering of eyelashes. Whatever age they are it's the same story. Look at my mother with her wretched parties and her hostess act – pretending it's her duty to flirt and gratify all the little whims of her goggling guests. A load of sucker babies. She thinks it's all part of the patronage system, all 'doing good'. The reality is, all women are secret whores. You Freudians I suppose would call it female masochism. It's innate. It's no different with Ophelia and all her fake-modest airs and graces. *Smile, nod, amble, jig, nickname.* The female act. Does she think I'm some ignorant fool who doesn't know anything about her past goings-on or her present ones for that matter? Or doesn't she care, so long as the façade of courtship is paced out in the approved manner?"

I was impressed by the impact Ophelia seemed to have made on him, which I had certainly not expected from his earlier detached, quizzical descriptions of a rather withdrawn figure who had seemed a mere appendage of her brother. I found myself suddenly curious to know what she was really like. Again I showed Hamlet his identification with the aggressive aspect of the Ghost-pilot as it appeared in his Batman dream, his contemptuous speech about women as secret whores, and indeed his own clothing. This was the domineering and status-conscious side of the fighter-pilot rather than the protective side. The implication seemed to be that his father, with his old-fashioned methods of wooing and conquering, would have no difficulty in flying through "paraphernalia" and "cobwebs" – in fact would have known how to make use of them as part of his own equipment for satisfying his desires. *With martial stalk.*

"That's Claude's obsession, more like", observed Hamlet sarcastically. "But Claude's methods are more slimy, less energetic. And my mother panders to him – compensation I suppose for flirting with all her other riff-raff. She's a fool."

The Batman dream should be taken as a warning, I said. It showed us the significance of acting-out, dressing up to imitate the Ghost-pilot-daddy; indeed, getting inside this aggressive aeroplane-daddy and his penis in the sense of a weapon. We could understand better now what had at first been puzzling in the Ghost's mention of revenge. The concept of revenge, I reminded him, had come up in response to Hamlet's reiterated question about what he should "do". Revenge was the answer to the desire for action – demonstrated clearly in the Batman dream.

"Surely", objected Hamlet, "the point is, what *kind* of action? You can't say all action is bad, all action is vengeful. You might as well say all sex is bad, so all we are allowed to do is think about it."

The distinction presented by the dreams, I explained, was a very fundamental one between action and communication. Action was really acting-out – acting on somebody or their feelings, manipulating them. In the Batman dream, for example, there was clearly no communication to communicate anything to Ophelia, but simply to conquer by action.

"That's because I knew *she'd* want it that way", he protested. "Like all women, she's a devout romancer. It goes with deviousness. I told you, I don't go for that primitive stuff myself, it's ludicrous. You don't believe the height of my ambition is to play Batman in the movies, do you?" he sneered.

As a dream-image, I said, it was no more ludicrous than that of the Ghost-pilot. It conveyed a meaning, which need not be literally translated into shinning up a drainpipe – there were other forms of action on Ophelia that he might find himself taking. Or possibly on his mother, as the Ghost had suggested; for we seemed to be dealing generally with the question of his attitude to women. The Ghost's implication was that, motivated by revenge against women, he might taint his own mind. This was the sort of action we needed to guard against.

"You know Dr Horacio, you have such an overdramatic view of my character", said he condescendingly. "You'd think I went around with a pocketful of hand-grenades. Consider – I am a peace-loving intellectual. I only fight when justifiably aroused. Even at school that was my reputation. Nobody can call me a coward – but I'm not an aggressor either. And certainly not against the weaker sex! *But*", he added in a harsh and ugly tone, "I'm not prepared to be played on by Ophelia's goody-goody masochism either. I'm not going to be teased into acting the sadist just to satisfy her feminine fantasies. She can bloody well take me as I am or not at all. Honesty is all I ask."

Uneasy at his unwillingness to be put in touch with the violence of his own feelings, I stressed again the importance of continuously examining his own motives in terms of action versus communication. And this time, instead of replying instantly, he reached into his jacket pocket and extracted not a hand-grenade but a folded piece of paper.

"I can see", he announced, "that nothing less than the oracular proof will satisfy you. Shall I read you the poem I sent Ophelia? Then you'll see that I do nothing without communication. It's private obviously but you're different."

He rather caught me by surprise, and I began to demur, but he was already reciting:

> O fuck fuck fuck,
> with words words words
> you play on me, and seem to know my
> stops.
> But if only my finger and tongue could
> govern your ventages,
> you'd see what excellent music would sound
> from the top to the bottom
> from this little organ
> at the heart of my
> mystery.

O dark, dark, dark. My heart was sinking as he read; I imagined his offputting effect on Ophelia and on her behalf I felt anxious to enable him to find some way of containing himself. *The most beautified Ophelia.* The poem, I told him, was a good illustration of what we had been talking about – action disguised as communication. *Beautified is a vile phrase.* This was his translation into real life of the action of the Batman dream – the fucking, wordplaying aspect of himself that believed all it had to do was "govern the ventages" like a pipe in order to penetrate the music of the mystery.

"How can you say that?" he complained, sounding a little crushed, "when it's a straightforward plea for an equal relationship?"

In an equal relationship, I said, neither person should be merely a pipe to be played on; it would be necessary to imagine the other as also having mystery. At the beginning of the session he had leapt to conclusions about hypocrisy, instead of admitting that he didn't understand Ophelia's intentions towards him. But instead of trying to gauge her state of mind, he had allowed himself to become inflamed and to act the Ghost by means of this letter.

"You just don't like the sexual explicitness in the poetic ambiguity", he declared, recovering his poise. "It's too arty for you. You wouldn't mind if it was a dream. Poems shouldn't be subject to moral censorship, that's their *raison d'etre*. They push the bounds. Even the most private sentiments achieve universality. That's why I'm going to publish it in *Varsity* next week."

I realized then that it was no use his bringing his poems here for interpretation as if they were dreams; in fact, it was probably counterproductive. I explained that his poetry was liable to be censored or arranged by himself, whereas a dream could speak directly to us about the processes of his inner world. For our purposes, a dream was explicit and a poem was not.

"Well if you don't approve of arranging material", he countered accusingly, "perhaps you should consider more closely what it is that you're doing with my dreams when you put them in one of your scientific papers. Aren't you just arranging them to suit yourself? I suppose you want to be the only person credited with talent."

The dream, I explained, was always his dream, as he had reported it, in no way tampered with; my interpretation of it and of the whole analytic situation could perhaps be called my dream of his dream. This applied to the transference between us in the sessions just as much as to scientific papers, should I ever include his material in those.

"*Your* dream", he repeated, with a guarded, surly spark of interest; "that's more like it, yeah!"

Nevertheless, he spent the last minutes of the session in a huff, grumbling about my sophistry, and he left with some sour mutterings.

I recognized that the setting of boundaries had become of particular importance. There was a confusion in his mind between intrusiveness and intimacy, public and private, action and contemplation. Hence he assumed that publishing the private poem to Ophelia was equivalent to my publishing his dreams – a type of offloading of projections. *For your desire to know what is between us, overmaster it as best you can.* I had my first hints of the enclosed, claustrophobic form that his grandiosity could take, and how this fed on the delusion that he was acting for his real father rather than his usurping uncle-father. He saw his mission as correcting the distorted vision or values of his mother. The confusions adumbrated during these first few weeks dominated the first term of our brief period of analysis and came to a head eventually on the field of battle, which we were to call "the Mousetrap".

Meanwhile, as I took my customary lunchtime walk on the Heath the day of the Batman session, I meditated on certain feelings of my own, which had begun through Hamlet to percolate my consciousness. The weather was cold and blustery with scudding clouds, the beginning of the gales that would sweep the leaves from the trees, now still laden with autumn colour. I walked down the hill as far as the pond above South End Green and paused on the causeway across it, leaning on the rail to watch the turbulence on the water. In the past, Beatrice had often used to come on these lunchtime walks, especially in the days when we lived in South End Green ourselves. Now she never did. We had moved up the hill to the affluent heart of Hampstead; but she had rented a share in a studio in Hackney and was rarely at home during the day. This was after she had accused me of ignoring her needs and undermining her by treating her as an ideal, a fiction of my own brain, rather than a person. At the time I could not imagine what she meant, so was sure she was wrong. I assumed she just needed to be released from the house, now that the girls could travel independently to school. But now, I could see that I was already developing an idealized view of Ophelia, in reaction to Hamlet's confusions; and I began to suspect that my over-romantic view of women was perhaps not something to be proud of but, on the contrary, was unconstructive, a type of self-indulgence. As though I implicitly believed women could not be trusted to have unpleasant feelings. I wondered, as I walked back up the side of East Heath Road, if it was possible that Beatrice actually disliked me at times, and if so, when did it start?

As a result of these troubled musings, I told myself I must not be overprotective of Hamlet's relationship with Ophelia, or indeed with his parents. I must allow him to make his own discoveries, not contaminated by ideals of my own, which were themselves in turbulence. If only, in the months ahead, I had been able to heed my own advice. But I was overtaken by the rapidity of events.

CHAPTER THREE

The Prince

> **Ophelia**: He rais'd a sigh so piteous and profound
> As it did seem to shatter all his bulk
> And end his being. That done, he lets me go,
> And with his head over his shoulder turn'd
> He seem'd to find his way without his eyes,
> For out o' doors he went without their helps,
> And to the last bended their light on me. (II. i. 94-100)

Hamlet's claustrophobic anxiety becomes clear in the context of his parents moving house. It takes the form of using Ophelia as his tool to attack his parent figures and their value systems.

Looks like the old devil was right about women being untrustworthy and two-faced, were Hamlet's opening words next session. I realized, of course, he was talking about the Ghost and Ophelia, and wondered what had transpired over the weekend. "The whole question is, which side expresses a woman's true nature – the inside or the outside", he said aggressively. *God has given them one face and they make themselves another.*

I thought this sounded ominous, and asked him to explain.

"And I'm asking you – what the fuck is this thing called beauty anyway?" he declaimed, gesticulating with his hands. *A bawd.* I saw he was about to deliver a tirade. "Fools say, the world is so beautiful, in their usual twittering plebspeak" (he mimicked a high idiotic whine). "What the hell does it really mean? Nothing – nothing it all. To mask the emptiness of their minds, and their tightarsed suburban inhibitions, people go about labelling things as beautiful just to show they're respectable and agree with each other. They all want to be part of the same mutual brainwashing system. That's all they need to give them a buzz. *The beauty of the world, the paragon of animals.* And it's exactly the same when it comes to women. Everyone is conditioned like Pavlov's dogs to start slavering at the sight of what is called a beautiful woman. But what is there really, underneath it all? *Nothing but a pestilent congregation of vapours.* A meaningless mess – phobias and perversions. But has anybody got the guts to admit it? Oh no, we're all supposed to keep up the show – keep it up, yeah, keep it up!"

He was fuming with sanctimonious rage. I suspected that much of this might be some sort of backlash from a sexual experience with Ophelia, about which he had said nothing so far. Even so I was surprised and somewhat incensed by this attack. I told Hamlet it was not the social conditioning of fashionable stereotypes which had aroused his violent ambivalence, but a subjective response which he felt was outside his control. He remained firmly ensconced in his aggressive, macho, Batman position.

He waited for me to finish my sentence, but scarcely listened to what I was saying, and as soon as I drew breath he launched into the second half of his speech:

"And as for truth – that's another social delusion, in fact a political one, even more pernicious. Professor Polly and his essay titles! I can see him now, walking backwards and forwards on the lecture platform, waving his arms in the pompous way he does when he's unloading his arthritic maxims. 'The truth', says he, wagging his finger in the air – 'the truth is a direction which can only be found by indirections!' *By indirections find directions out.* Ros and Gil were convulsed. Polly didn't notice – or if he did he'd have thought it was a sign of their youthful enthusiasm – following their worthy professor on the track of a 'truly scientific means of philosophical investigation of psychological structures!' *Words, words, words.* So on he goes, hunting the trail of policy as he calls it, and 'excavating the truth which is buried in the secret core of the mountain of evidence'. And all this crap delivered with such a naive, bright-eyed beaver look about him, as if he really believed he was on to some worldshaking discovery! *Buzz, buzz, buzz.* Well now I've found *him* out instead. Coleridge understood his type – a man of maxims rather than of ideas. Not an idea in his entire babyhead." *A great baby – a capital calf.*

It was clear to me from all this, of course, that Hamlet's initial admiration for Professor Polack had switched suddenly to a virulent contempt, paralleling the switch in his attitude to his own father indicated by the Ghost dream. Stung by the suddenness and intensity of this attack, and at a loss to explain it, I asked Hamlet if the Professor had recently made any harsh criticisms of his academic work?

"God no", replied Hamlet scathingly, "not Polly - nothing but mindless praise from him, even when I write an essay as lousy as the last one. I can tell it's lousy – he can't. His last precious word of advice to us – believe it or not – was 'Brevity is the soul of wit.' As if he had any idea what brevity was! No, he's completely past it."

It was hard to assess to what extent Hamlet was exaggerating with his satirical treatment of the Professor. I remembered his parents' statement about Polack's high opinion of Hamlet's work. Possibly Hamlet was disappointed in his own estimation of it as a search for truth. Clearly there was a connection between this "truth" and the hidden core of feminine beauty which had enraged him as being disappointing or unattainable. I asked Hamlet if Polack had shown signs of disapproval over his interest in Ophelia?

"Why should he?" he said, surprised. "Anyway, Ophelia can twist him round her little finger. He thinks he's in charge of her but really she's in charge of him."

So as I suspected, the genesis of Hamlet's revulsion was to be found only within himself. I put it to him that once he was convinced of Polack's admiration for him, he decided the Professor must be an idiot, a "baby" who he had been fooling the whole time with his clever antics. He felt he had been leading the Professor round in "indirections". Not Ophelia, but he, had been twisting him round his finger. In effect he was accusing himself of being an imposter, and Polack of being a fool not to recognize it. He felt himself to be an intruder in this mysterious value-system of truth-and-beauty. *The bawdlike commerce of beauty and honesty.* The problem still remained of whether he was an imposter in the sphere of his work, or of Ophelia, or both?

"Hang on", he objected, irritated, "now *you're* the one who's twisting! I was talking about how decrepit and unreliable Polly's judgement has become – his day is over. Mostly my essays are bloody good. It was only the last one that got infected by his own mumblings, I couldn't get them out of my head, like a virus in the brain. *Tragical-comical-historical-pastoral or poem unlimited.*"

Nonetheless, I insisted, Polack's main folly – according to Hamlet – seemed to be to "believe in" Hamlet and his truth. This was the gist of his account. He accused the Professor of misleading through "words, words, words". Yet as we knew, Hamlet's own gift of the gab could be an equally unreliable vehicle for truth. *Whorelike unpacking the heart with words.* The suggestion here was that he had been using words as a camouflage for indirect or intrusive entry into a world where he felt he had no place, no honest business. *In the ear of their conference.*

"My whole point", protested Hamlet in aggrieved tones, "is that there *is no* truth – there is no such thing. It's an outdated concept, a form of brainwashing." *Doubt truth to be a liar.*

The truth we were talking about here, I said, was the sincerity of his feelings and motivation – in relation possibly to his work, certainly to Ophelia.

"So – what is it he really wants to know?" Hamlet finally exploded. "That I've been having it off with his precious daughter? So what – is that a truth? It's no big deal, there's no mystery behind that. It's just that Polly likes to get his information through hints and circumlocutions. He has to make a baby-faced detective game out of it, an easter-egg hunt. Unless it's wrapped up in a secret to start with there's no satisfaction in the discovery."

Perhaps, I said, this particular mode of insincerity was one which applied to Hamlet himself. I pointed out that his method of informing me he had commenced sexual relations with Ophelia was itself a circuitous one.

"I didn't realize you were in such a hurry to know", he responded sarcastically.

His anxiety was, then, that he had used false or caricatural means to gain entry to Ophelia, holding her hostage before her father. Unable to tolerate the disturbing effect her beauty had on him, he had tried to capture or conquer it. In his hostage-holding technique there was, of course, an abuse of trust in relation to all involved.

"If anything it's me who's the hostage in that set-up", said Hamlet. "She's her daddy's girl and I'm on probation."

Possibly, then, her beauty was aggravated in Hamlet's eyes by her closeness to her father. Unsure of his own position, he became suspicious that she was just her father's tool, a decoy used to betray his inmost "secrets" to the Professor. He felt trapped, essentially, by the confusing effect that beauty had on men's judgement.

"It's not her looks I'm suspicious about", said Hamlet; "it's the way she uses them – not just with me, with everybody." *How to interpret between her and her love.*

Exactly, I confirmed. Her beauty was obvious to everybody; but the *meaning* of her beauty – that is, her feelings about Hamlet in particular - was not at all obvious. Hence his disturbance and frustration.

"I told you that myself", he said with disdain. "With women, the outside is no guide to the inside."

And now, I told him, he had found that sexual activity in itself was not the key to this mystery, not a magical solution.

Possessing the beautiful object did not in itself lead to the truth about either himself or Ophelia.

"You're really just an oldfashioned moralist, Dr Horacio, aren't you", he said. "I mean, there's nothing new in all this talk, is there? The beautiful object – the sacred cow."

His persistent scorn and irritation now began to make sense. His denigration of beauty, I said, was a way of denying the humiliation of an experience of impotence. The splitting of Ophelia into inside and outside, upper and lower parts of the body, paralleled his splitting of his father into good and bad, heroic and degenerate, Hyperion and a satyr. By this means a degree of contempt for Ophelia had crept in to his view of her; and this, I suggested, was in fact the cause of the impotence.

Hamlet shrugged this off, as he left the session, with a quiet, laconic cynicism. Something about this perturbed me even more than his raging. He clearly found the humiliation unbearable; and his glib sophistical slickness disguised, I could see, a deep failure of emotional contact. I suspected that Ophelia was becoming the new focus for his ambivalence – his love and his antagonism – superseding his parents and Polack. And his attacks on beauty and truth, which were now to be directed toward this vulnerable girl, wounded me deeply, so that I felt the urge to rise to her defence. The fighter-pilot stirred within me. Nevertheless I told myself, yet again, not to try to push the young couple together. Their relationship must evolve of itself. I must stand back despite Hamlet's pressure to turn me into either the pilot or Polack. *Be not passion's slave.*

One Monday morning a few sessions after this, Hamlet clomped down the steps in a filthy temper, bumping into walls and doorjambs with uncharacteristic clumsiness (normally he moved like a cat, quick and lithe). As he entered the room he gave the carpet a vicious jab with the toe of his boot where it was slightly loose at the door junction, rucking it up.

"Why the hell can't you get this place fixed", he muttered; "it's the pits." He lay down with his hands still firmly ensconced in the pockets of his jacket, elbows sticking out, and announced:

"Well, Claude's chucked me out of the house at last."

I was, as he knew, aware that his parents were in the process of moving out of their large house to a smaller flat, also in Hampstead – his father having decided to retire early from his business. After an impressive pause filled with silent indignation, he complained:

"They've found themselves a place where there couldn't possibly be room for me. A bijou residence! I told Claude of course – because I can't stand his way of secretly fiddling things behind my back – that I got the message completely. In fact I was glad to have it out in the open."

I asked, did he not have a room of his own in the new flat?

"A room! A *room*", he snorted morosely. "Oh yeah – a room. I've been allocated a sort of cupboard half way up the stairs, about the size of a hamster cage. *Nose me as you go up the stairs into the lobby.* And my mother babbles on about how they're going to have a skylight put in and fitted furniture and how it'll be ideal for me when I come home. When I come home! They'll be lucky."

I pointed out the claustrophobic anxiety behind his sense of dispossession – enclosed and shut away by his parents in the hamster cage, while "fiddling" was going on behind his back. It was reminiscent of the Ghost's complaint about weaning. There was also some envy of his parents' nest-building (which I related to the way he had scuffed my carpet); and a denial of his anxiety about why they needed to move – Claude's illness in particular.

"Nest-building!" he said contemptuously. "Behind my back – at their age – it's disgusting. Why do you think they chose the middle of the term to do it in, when I'm tied up at Cambridge? The fact is, the silly woman can't see through any of this – whatever Claude arranges, she raves over. Anything to keep him happy. That's a Pavlovian response for you. She's blinded by her own libido. *Mutiny in a matron's bones. Refrain tonight* – some chance. So long as there's a place for their king-size bed, and a sitting room big enough for entertaining their legions of fascinating guests, everything is "super duper"! What a phrase. According to *her*, it's going to be "so much better, so much less to worry about" – all words Claude has put into her mouth only she doesn't realize it, to disguise the fact that what he wants is to get me out the way." *Ship him hence.*

This speech was delivered on a note of vitriolic outrage, and after a second's pause, Hamlet concluded: "No, I really can't stand Claude's style – it's suffocating. The bourgeois patriarch squatting at the centre of his web like some great fat spider. *With an auspicious and a drooping eye.* Quite honestly, I'm glad to quit."

This time, I connected Hamlet's fury and anxiety at being unhoused, thrown out, with the episode of impotence which he had been too humiliated to confirm. This also was generated by his Batman identification with an aggressively patriarchal figure, ruler of women and the home, which made him feel suffocated, imprisoned. *Denmark's a prison.*

"Don't worry", said Hamlet, again ignoring my interpretation. "I'm taking steps to get out. I'm not one to bear a grudge, and I can see – our ways must part. I mean, there's no point sitting brooding like a constipated chicken, waiting for my uncle to change his spots. I can't live on air. *A capon, promise-crammed.* I need my freedom of interpretation. And now is my chance to catch the old goat at his own game, so everybody can see what's really going on. *Her*, in particular!"

The edge of excitement creeping into his voice was always an ominous sign, as was this talk about "freedom of interpretation" and "getting out", in the context of his enclosed, anxious state. What, I asked him suspiciously, was "really going on" in his view?

"Well the upshot is" – he began with a certain triumph, "I've had it out with old Polly and I'm going to be producing the Shakespeare play at the end of term. And when my mother sees it – hell, will it blow her mind! *Blow it to the moon.* At last they'll see it how it really is. Even Claude's eyes might be opened – if he can blink in his brutish haze."

His zealous manner was giving me twinges of anxiety even before he confessed that whatever he had in mind was to be directed explicitly against his parents. Which play was it? I asked – for some reason, thinking of *Othello*.

"Believe it or not", he said, "it's *A Midsummer Night's Dream*. A surprising choice for me, you might think – a play for babies really. But you'd be amazed at the dark and bestial fantasies there are hidden underneath all that fairy stuff. If you dig deep enough you can really blow them at the moon!" Then he told me, with satisfaction, how Ophelia had agreed to be Titania and to perform a song-and-dance act from *Cabaret* which he had inserted. *A speech of some dozen or sixteen lines.* Her brother, though, had refused to act the part of one of her attendants: "I tried to explain that in *my Dream*, which for Christ's sake is a *Dream* of 1973, I don't need fairies who are little ballet-girls, I need big hulking men and he'd have been perfect. What the hell - I've got Rosenfeld and Gildstein down instead for Peaseblossom and Cobweb, and a couple of first years – Peacock and Seaman – for Moth and Mustardseed. They're all going to double as the mechanicals, to bring out the ambiguity of the whole thing. I'm going to do Bottom myself, of course. You don't know it but he's the hero, he flips them top to bottom. *Hoist on their own petard.* That's the basic set-up already. The art, you see, lies in getting the right people teamed up to express my message."

As I listened to his "basic set-up", not just foreboding but anger was rising in me. He was converting the play into some sort of omnipotent masturbatory phantasy founded on big hulking mechanical-fairy-fingers. Now it was Shakespeare's turn to be held hostage. But that in itself was the least of my worries. I was disturbed by the mixture of sanctimony and violence in his language – such as "blowing at the moon" and "blowing his mother's mind'; and even more, by the public acting-out of this phantasy with himself and Ophelia in fixed positions at the centre of it all. In explaining this to Hamlet, I warned him of the possibility of damaging his private relationship with this girl.

"She's *my* girlfriend!" he protested, not so much possessively as authoritatively, in the manner of a young eighteenth-century aristocrat talking about his housemaid. I said that did not entitle him to treat her as his whore.

He laughed unpleasantly, a little surprised, and defended himself by saying: "I credited you with being more enlightened about the whole scene of sexual freedom. A radical staging like mine is bound to shock the older generation – some of them. You're obviously cramped by the same outdated values as the rest."

Slogans such as "sexual freedom" and "freedom of interpretation", I said, were banners for action and would contaminate his private relationships. It was the omnipotent "fuck, fuck" side of himself taking over again.

"What's the difference anyway between what you call my slogans (just because you don't like them) and your values, which are simply out of date (but I don't hold that against you)?" he demanded.

Values were a basis for communication between people, I explained; slogans were for imposing his will on people.

"Honour thy father and mother is what it boils down to, isn't it, according to you?" he sneered, as if even I must consider this value too degradingly simplistic, a *reductio ad absurdum*.

All right, I said with some impatience, he could consider honouring Shakespeare as a reasonable starting-point for his play production, and move on from there, instead of arranging everything and everybody around his own directorial role, to express his message as he put it. Shakespeare was after all the father of his own play, and the play had its own aesthetic dignity, not to be violated.

"Ah, so that's it after all!" he said in a tone of triumph, as if he had winkled the secret of my resistance out of me. "You just can't stomach my interpretation. I knew it! All this charade about psychoanalysis being a scientific process – now it turns out you're just a literary romantic after all. To you Shakespeare is some sort of god, not to be profaned by the realities of everyday life. You can't see he's simply one of the great hacks, churning out fodder for his patrons. The libidinal orgy they want to wallow in, he hands it over on a plate." *What's Hecuba to him, or he to her?*

And to my gloom and frustration, he left with his princely omnipotence not merely intact but inflamed. I saw that I had failed utterly to deflate it. And for a while after this, Hamlet seemed careful not to say too much about the play, although I was aware of it fulminating in the background. He clearly didn't want any interference, and developed a subtly condescending attitude to me, as if it were up to me to re-establish my status as his professional confidante after exceeding my brief. Correspondingly, he was meticulous about punctuality and other formal aspects of the analytic setting, but in a way which suggested this was really a substitute for true co-operation, a pretence to disguise his essential secretiveness. Moreover I could see that I, too, had become a hostage to his princely antics, now that he had, inevitably, discovered my own aesthetic values; and in this context it made me feel strangely vulnerable. I counselled myself to be more cautious for the time being and to wait for dreams. Hamlet was having difficulty remembering these, but eventually he did bring me an interesting and thoughtful dream which, despite its air of egocentricity, seemed to augur hopefully for his relationship with Ophelia. I began to believe this might escape damage from the play after all.

This dream, which we came to call the "To be or not to be" dream because it was about the question of "being" a lover, went as follows:

> *Doctor Horacio, I do not know*
> *Whether to fall in love, or not to fall*
> *In love. Sick with indecision,*
> *The current of my resolution's gone*
> *Awry. Was this the drink my father drank*
> *That shot him into a sky of troubles? - to taste*
> *The heartache and the thousand natural shocks*
> *That strike like lightning from the heart of life's*
> *Outrageous stormclouds, whose consummation*
> *Is only death. What dream can help me now,*
> *The ignorant survivor of his catastrophe?*
> *Suppose I shuffle off this mortal coil,*
> *My naked newborn soul can only pause*
> *In apprehension, puzzled as it stands*
> *On the cliff's brink, while all before, the world*
> *Spreads out into the misty distance. Why fly*
> *To sins as yet unknown - and should I jump,*
> *Or fall? And even as I stand and think,*
> *Her shaping spirit awakes my recollection*
> *Like a chill vapour of early dawn, and I pray*
> *That love and fame to nothingness will sink.*

"I know what the dream means", stated Hamlet with quiet confidence. "It means I really am in love with Ophelia after all. I was thinking that yesterday after the rehearsal. Rosenfeld said I was lucky to be going out with Ophelia, he wouldn't mind her himself – he was quite offhand, sort of joky, and walked straight off. But it made me think, yes, it was only natural everybody should want Ophelia. I really *was* lucky. And a sort of warm glow went through me – I felt strange, and sad. I thought, maybe we could really make it together."

Then he began to talk about the dream, and how "all that about consummation meant sex not death" and was about the sensuality in his family which he'd inherited but could accept better now, because he saw that Ophelia was beginning to suss him out and appreciate his complexities, even his hang-ups. Working together on the play made it clear that she really understood what he wanted her to do, and it was a fact that she was "fabulous – everybody said so". *A form in wax, by me imprinted.*

"It's Coleridge, you know, about shaping spirit," he informed me. "And that about love and fame is Keats – we've been doing them this term. I used to think, who wants Romantic wish-wash about moons and waterfalls when you could have compasses and telescopes like the Metaphysicals – which is so much more like real life. But now I see I can use them after all."

I noted the childish egocentricity which Hamlet's confidences in me still had, when he felt I was somehow "pleased" with him. It was an indication of his instability; he could easily swing back into manic arrogance. On the one hand I took him to mean that perhaps he could use me (the "old romantic") and my services. *Wear me in his heart's core.* On the other hand his enthusiasm for both Ophelia and the Romantic poets seemed to be grounded to some degree in the way in which he could "use" them in projects of his own, a form of manipulation through projective identification in relation to both Ophelia and the poets, rather than communicating or learning. He believed Ophelia understood him; I put it to him, had he ever considered whether he understood *her*? Similarly, he made judgements about the usefulness of poetic diction in "real life" (that is, to himself) without first considering whether he had first understood the poets' usage.

This lack of humility was characteristic of what I described to him as his "princely" mentality. It was, of course, directed toward me too: I was a member of his entourage, allotted a strictly limited function of observing and recording, receiving his confidences, but not allowed to curb his acting-out. That would be going too far – a type of indecorum. Thus he had fixed on Shakespeare's *Dream* and, pre-empting my role as interpreter of dreams, he handed over his own version to me as his amanuensis or scribe. *Observe mine uncle with your soul.* I pointed out to him that he was treating me as his future biographer, witness to the facts of his emotional display, while paralysing any effective intervention on my part. At this he laughed indulgently, taking it – from his prince's viewpoint – as a compliment to his management. Once again, I was the one left feeling hurt and vulnerable.

I returned, therefore, to the interpretation of his latest dream – which was, like all his dreams, full of emotional significance. I emphasized its importance first of all as a pause for thought which was both rare and welcome. *The dreams that give us pause.* Acting-out (the "current of resolution") was suspended in mid-air, allowing a breathing space. At that moment nothing was inevitable. The readymade channels down which action was supposed to plunge became "puzzled" (to use the dream's very evocative word). Hamlet's direction was no longer obvious, no longer propelled by slogans and sanctimony.

This meant also, however, that his position regarding falling in love was a tenuous and unresolved one. The picture in the dream was not quite the same as the warm glow he had described, a glow of satisfaction and possession, the triumph of having secured a desirable girl. The dream showed that in fact things were much more complicated. Here, love was associated with "shocks", "heartache", lightning, etc., and the implication was that his father seemed to have been prepared to face this emotional turbulence. It was an interesting variation on the theme of his father's heroism in the Ghost dream. Hamlet himself was maybe on the brink of such an experience, but he had not actually "jumped" as yet. *The will is puzzled.* His tentative puzzlement suggested a certain disappointment in his sense of gratifying Ophelia and in his own sexual gratification, which was not as immediate or overwhelming as he had expected. I pointed out to Hamlet that he was still very much a beginner in sexual love, and was only gradually discovering the complications and confusions which were involved in becoming a lover. *Honeying and making love in the nasty sty.*

It was, indeed, a very sensitive and revealing dream. Potentially it could be a great help to Hamlet in his relationship with his girlfriend. In my enthusiasm for the dream, however, I had overestimated Hamlet's capacity to tolerate any interpretation which seemed to him to undermine his princely dignity. Making the connection with the Ghost dream, and reminding Hamlet that in this area his stature was still as it were lower than his father's, nearly lost me my tenuous role as confidante.

"You wait till you see my play", he said coldly. "It puts all these chivalric hangups about love in a modern perspective. Claude and his type will be utterly deflated." (Was I, I wondered, now one of "his type"?) "You are coming to see it, aren't you?" he added suddenly, alarmed. I explained that I did not think it advisable.

"You'll miss something", he warned me, clearly disappointed. *Catching the conscience of the King, the Queen and all.*

I didn't doubt it. My curiosity to see Ophelia almost tempted me to consider creeping in secretly. This was, however, too risky, and was overridden by my caution over the boost I knew it would give to Hamlet's omnipotence should he find out, as he very likely would. In addition, I felt the play was wasting analytic time, providing an outlet for Hamlet's directorial or princely antics, without allowing us really to get our teeth into these in the analytic context. *Just half a fellowship in a cry of players.* Whenever we came across evidence of his omnipotence or egocentricity he would automatically take shelter in the play, as if this would provide the answer to everything. Anybody who saw his play, it was implied, would lose their oldfashioned inhibitions and receive enlightenment. The new prince would come into his own.

This time, as Hamlet passed me on his way out of the consulting room, he looked momentarily but intensely in my eyes and said, "You'll see, Dr Horacio, there are more things in heaven and earth than in your 'dreaming' philosophy. Bye for now." His dark smouldering glance, under the strips of lanky dark hair falling vertically over his cheeks, gave me a sense of extreme foreboding. *This bodes some strange eruption to our state.* I told myself to prepare for some volcanic eruption in his state of mind.

CHAPTER FOUR

The Mousetrap

> **Ophelia**: You are as good as a chorus, my lord.
> **Hamlet**: I could interpret between you and your love
>   if I could see the puppets dallying.
> **Ophelia**: You are keen, my lord, you are keen.
> **Hamlet**: It would cost you a groaning to take off my edge.
> **Ophelia**: Still better, and worse.
> **Hamlet**: So you mis-take your husbands. – Begin,
>   murderer. (III .ii. 240-46)

Hamlet has stung Horacio into losing his grip on the analytic transference, and Horacio is astounded by news of Ophelia's pregnancy. After the Mousetrap dream however Horacio appreciates Hamlet's vulnerability and for the time being the analysis is back on track.

It was Hamlet himself who first described his version of Shakespeare's *Midsummer Night's Dream* as a "mousetrap" intended to exhibit to his parents the stupid and pornographic nature of their lovemaking. (It transpired that in fact Claude was in the habit of calling Gertrude his "mouse".) *Pinch wanton on her cheek, call her his mouse.* By the end of this play production, however, every member of our little drama had sustained some degree of insult or injury.

"There's a political message here", he explained to me, during one of his compulsive lectures, when I had to exercise all my ingenuity to get a word in edgewise. "You could say I'm a man with a mission. I need a play that I can take off in – and to take shape, the play needs me. That's the wonderful thing about poetry. It cries out to be rewritten by succeeding generations. Now that notions of authorial Authority have been discredited, new poets like me are faced with the public duty of altering the old bard's canon to suit ourselves. That, of course, is the challenge. People should thank their lucky stars there's someone like me around who can strip the tinsel wrapping off this play and expose the secret bestiality of the affair. You've got to be cruel to be kind." *Reform, reform it altogether.*

These were terrorist tactics, I told him, with their characteristic mixture of sanctimony and complacency. I had tried repeatedly to warn Hamlet of the danger of taking "revenge" on his objects through manic enactments. His talk of being a "man with a mission" and "taking off" in the play demonstrated acting-out on the lines of the Batman dream – the aggressive aspect of the Ghost-pilot. In the Ghost dream he had been so confused with his father's penis he could not distinguish whether it was heroic or assaultive. Now he was acting as though he were living inside it, taking military action on what he had called this "play for babies". The play was Shakespeare's baby and he was holding it hostage in order to attack his parents.

"You sound like Polly with your worshipful phraseology", he said, evidently trying to restrain the contempt in his voice, *de haut en bas*. "This isn't the classroom, it's the stage. It's worship that results in the death of art. Until I give this play an audience and make it relevant to the complex issues of today, it's going to stay mummified in the attic of English Heritage to be guarded by fossils like Professor Polly!"

And so, for many sessions, I made fruitless attempts to penetrate the sanctimony of what he called his mission, and put him back in touch with the ambivalence and hostility toward the aesthetic which had come out clearly in his tirades against "truth and beauty". Whenever I made any headway with this he became irritable and contemptuous, and put me in my place; then – probably the next session – he would be furtive and a little anxious, surreptitiously seeking reassurance that he hadn't in fact made an enemy of me. But the actual content of my "sermonizing" (as he put it) slipped over him like water off a duck's back, making no emotional contact and I felt deskilled. I reflected on the particular difficulty I had with Hamlet in describing the transference without the help of dreams. Unless a dream was in front of us, with its graphic evidence for the transference, it was easy to be seduced into the conflictual debating mode which he invited, and then the emotionality of our relationship was dissipated.

To one of those "furtive" sessions, at last, he brought an odd little dream about *a huge old yew tree growing in an enclosure with steps and a stone balustrade in front and a stately building in the background (reminding him of the Fitzwilliam museum). From inside the tree came a strange wailing voice, crying urgently at regular intervals, "Set me free, set me free!" At last the warden came along, unlocked the gate into the enclosure, and tapped the tree with his stick, upon which a small creature like a squirrel emerged from an opening in the bark and darted quickly away. But then the warden appeared distraught, and ran round the tree in circles, crying "My money, my daughter! My money, my daughter!"* In the dream this had not seemed comical, but a logical way of addressing some serious problem.

Hamlet told me that the tree with steps and the stately facade resembled the stageset for his play, and that the warden, who was bald with a pointed beard, reminded him of Professor Polack. I could see that the dream had something to do with his claustrophobia and with the release of trapped femininity, but it was hard to say whether the Professor-warden was the imprisoner, or the liberator, or both. *It was his art made gape the pine and let out Ariel.* Hamlet had not long ago described him sarcastically as a "guardian" of literature; hence the association with the Museum; but this also suggested an uncreative, sterile guardianship, perhaps linked with the idea more of money than of daughter. *My ducats, my daughter.* The warden's words about his money and his daughter also took us back to the "chocolate box" dream at the beginning of his analysis, in which the Professor had exhorted his children to "grow and prosper". *For he did dream of money-bags.* In that dream there was a similar ambiguity about the idea of prosperity – did this mean growth and development, or did it mean wealth and success?

"That's Polly all right", said Hamlet sarcastically. "It's hard to tell which is his greater obsession – whether he owns Shakespeare or Ophelia." And he admitted that he had had an altercation with the Professor after he had come to see the dress rehearsal of his production. "Well what can you expect at his age?" he shrugged, with casual disdain. "His opinions are all fuddled up – he liked this, but then he didn't like that, and then again … blah blah."

I interpreted that it was me, not just Polack, whom he was attacking for having a proprietary attitude toward both the play and Ophelia. The warden was a tragic-comic figure presented like Shylock the Jew, taken to be envious of his own family's wealth, garnering gleanings from their outskirts. *Why should the poor be flattered?* I was also, of course, the guardian of psychoanalysis. Therein lay my "money-bags". The dream confirmed the location of our current problem in the realm of aesthetic vitality, and the need for the aesthetic object to have its freedom. This was our constant theme in the context of the Play as an aesthetic, feminine object, in which resided Hamlet's own femininity – linked also with his relation to Ophelia.

At this, Hamlet turned his head and said aggressively, raising his hand in an oratorical gesture:

"The fact is, Dr Horacio, you've got such fixed notions about this fucking play, that in spite of going on about it incessantly, you can't even be bothered to come and see my production." *Guilty creatures sitting at a play.*

I explained again that it would be inappropriate for me to come and see it – it was better for him to talk to me about it. With a play, he retorted, "everything was in the context and the staging" and my enslavement to the domination of words was as bad as Polly's: "If you actually came to *see* it – especially the way Ophelia does it – you'd be knocked out!"

With sinking heart I asked him again to describe it, reproaching myself for my cowardice in having hoped it might blow over without my having to hear too much about it.

"All right", he began, with defiance and a certain pomposity. *Leave thy damnable faces and begin.* "You have to realize, to start off with, that the core of the whole thing is the scenes between Bottom and Titania in the wood, and the wood of course is the facade for a brothel, a high-class bordello, and it's the place where all these Athenian aristocrats go to learn about sex and how to do it – that's why they can't get married till they've been there. Snakes with double tongues and enamelled skin, thickets and bushes of pubic hair, streakings of magic juice – it's all code for sexual parts. The fairies are there for the foreplay, to oil the process and get it all working – sucking out honey-bags, lighting thighs with glow-worms ... I mean, you've only got to look at those names – Squash, Peascod, Mustardseed. Titania calls it "doing courtesies". So the fairies are all sex aids – that's why I've got them doubling with the mechanicals; they're dressed up in rugby gear and they do a brilliant song and dance routine with Titania, a kind of classy strip act – you ought to see it, I mean really. When Bottom comes along it's all jazzed up because the fairies are in *his* service then, so he can use them to service Titania. Titania, you see, is still a virgin and that's why she's pissed off with Oberon – he's impotent (which explains why he's so obsessed with the drugs scene). So once she's found a real man, who wears his balls on his head (his arse-head of course) she closes her trap on him. *What monsters they make of us.* And like he says, he hasn't got "wit enough to get out of this wood" – he's stuck between her legs with his "tongue tied up", that is his prick. *A thought to lie between maids' legs.* He doesn't mind, of course – he's game for anything. And *she* doesn't care if he's some stupid labourer – that's all the better, in fact she wants to enslave herself to him:

> I will purge thy mortal grossness so,
> That thou shalt like an airy spirit go –

she says to Bottom – that's code for the male orgasm of course, "purging". Then there's her coy moan about the moon's "watery eye" which makes "every little flower" weep (and it's obvious what that means), "lamenting some enforced chastity". The fact is of course she's dying to have her chastity enforced, and that's what Bottom does for her –

> "So doth the woodbine the sweet honeysuckle
> Gently entwist; the female ivy so
> Enrings the barky fingers of the elm."

Barky fingers – so long as it's twisting up her she'll ring her muscles round it, and there you have the female orgasm! So long as it's barky she's happy – that's Shakespearean ambiguity for you", he finished in a triumphant and provocative manner. *Reechy kisses.*

And indeed, I found I was provoked. *His words like daggers entered in my ears.* It was now crystal clear that what had started as an act of "revenge" on his parents, trying to split them through ridiculing their sexuality, had switched its focus like a spotlight onto Ophelia. *A show with puppets dallying.* She was now the primary victim of his abusive phantasy, and all the macho obscenity of his interpretation of the play was directed at her, holding her up in the eyes of everyone as his whore. I didn't need to see the play, I said, to realize from his description that his antagonism was also directed at the analysis, displaying for ridicule the world of the dream and my role as the dream-interpreter.

"Oh God – this really is too boring, Dr Horacio", was his derisive response to my anxieties. "I can't understand why it bugs you so much. Whose reputation is it you're worrying about anyway? It's me not you who's on the line. As for Ophelia – she *wants* to be in it, I'm not forcing her. It's the ideal vehicle for her talents."

I told him he was completely oblivious to the contempt he was displaying for Ophelia, presenting her as slave to his sexual manipulations. It was the same as making Shakespeare's play the victim of his directorial twistings – the "indirections" of the intruder, ensconced in this identification with an aggressive princely penis. This was not Shakespearean ambiguity but an imposition of his own: a mousetrap in which everyone was caught – his parents, his girlfriend, Shakespeare, and the analysis itself.

He swore agitatedly and said, "At last I've got the chance to do something really creative and all you lot can do is shit on it! Well – all I can say is, dirtymindedness is in the eye of the beholder!"

And he departed in high dudgeon, looking daggers at me.

Shortly after this the play p roduction was over, and now the Christmas break was approaching. Hamlet appeared at the last Saturday session with a manic, self-righteous gleam in his eyes. He was wearing a heavy, mayoresque chain over his black jacket. He hardly glanced at me as he strode in with tight-set lips, flung himself on the couch and commenced one of his tirades.

"Believe it or not, Her Royal Highness summoned me last night to an exclusive interview in her private apartments. Naturally I was most gratified, given my humble status as the household cat, to be vouchsafed this rare and privileged opportunity for a few intimate words alone with my mother. After all, she never noticed my existence when we actually lived together – *much* too busy for that – though she's obviously found plenty of time to jabber to old Polly and the rest of her retinue *about* me! As for High and Mighty himself – he was skulking somewhere out of sight, as he always does when there's anything unpleasant going on. So much for his patriarchal guts." *A rat, a rat.*

Hamlet then explained that he had gone to his parents' flat after his last session, not intending to stay the night, but to pick up some things to take to Nando's and to get something to eat "because there's never any grub at his place". His parents, he knew, were out with friends watching "some slushy Bergman film" at the Everyman cinema. "They're all fascinated by each others' degenerating marriages – it saves looking more closely at their own." *A mirror to nature.* Then as he was about to leave the house his mother had returned, alone "or pretending to be", and insisted on speaking to him.

"'Hamlet my dear', she begins" (he began), "'I have been wanting to speak to you for a while' (well who's been stopping you?), 'but it's been hard to know how to approach the subject – you've been so much leading your own life lately' (yes I have had a bit on my mind – moving my gear into Forte and Nando's for a start, 'cos I can't stand the Bijou Residence any longer even for the vac). Then she starts whingeing at me in that typical nauseating female way. *Jig, amble and lisp*. 'These have, of course, been rather difficult times for all of us' (oh yeah?) 'and it is imperative to pay it some serious thought' (good, good – very glad, I'm all in favour of serious thought – can she possibly have noticed there is more to life than fornication?). Next, I have to listen to how she, and Claude, and Polly, have all been worrying about my behaviour (that is, gossiping about me behind my back – thank you, dear Mother, I am most flattered to be the object of your dedicated attention, so much in demand by all and sundry – Sundry in particular). *O wonderful son that can so 'stonish a mother*. And finally, she draws herself up to her full height of five foot three, and makes the magisterial pronouncement: 'My dear Hamlet, we really must discuss what is to be done – you are no longer a child, and neither is she.'"

These words struck me with a grey foreboding as I sensed we were getting to the point, but Hamlet continued with his circuitous rant:

"Then off again into all this twaddle about serious intentions and feminine feelings and other wish-wash that I suppose she gets from films and novels – such is the insatiable appetite of the female sex for sentimental slurp! *They have made me mad*. I tried to get it across to her that *my* feelings were real ones – doubtless beyond her comprehension – and that the subtleties of my mind had their existential profundity in what was quite simply space-aeons away from TV serials and Bergman mopies. *The trappings and the suits of woe*."

Here Hamlet paused for a moment to let the injured self-righteousness of his declaration sink into my consciousness. Now, I thought, he is finally going to tell me. Well? I asked.

"And then, only then –" he declared solemnly, "after all this bullshit, does she finally say to me: 'Perhaps you don't realize that Ophelia is pregnant?'"

Oh God, I thought.

"That was how she said it, the hypocrite – all smug and quiet, and with no warning at all – just to make a complete fool of me! Can you possibly understand my feelings? I very much doubt it. I could have hit her. I felt as though she'd hit *me*. I don't think I did hit her, I can't quite remember – perhaps I shook her by the shoulders or something, I felt sick with rage – literally, I thought I was going to vomit. I just remember rushing out and slamming the door."

I was dismayed at this unexpected blow, coming upon us at the worst possible time in the analysis. *When sorrows come, it's not as single spies, but in battalions.* Hamlet's murderous feelings were not being contained within the analytic context, but were erupting outside it, and yet he seemed oblivious of the implications of his violence. I realized (though he didn't) that Gertrude had been frightened of him, and with good reason. It was essential to bring him out of his sanctimonious cocoon and back into emotional contact. I warned Hamlet more emphatically than ever of the dangers of allowing himself to be taken over by the aggressive, anti-feminine masculinity of the Batman dream, and how this had very nearly resulted in actual violence against his mother.

He listened to my urgent interpretation with irritable impatience, and accused me of being seduced by his mother "like all the rest":

"You just can't see, can you', he said sourly, "that it's me who's the victim in all this, not my blasted mother. Do you suppose I was going to murder her, like some Gothic heroine? I'm entitled to my feelings too, you know. What do you think I am, a poker-faced cold fish like Forte or somebody?" (Forte, it appeared, being a friend of Nando's to whom Hamlet had taken a particular dislike.) Then he continued, more savagely: "And it's *her* fault as much as anyone's – yes, Ophelia's! another favourite of yours - she who in her beauty and innocence can do no wrong - unless of course corrupted by some worthless and depraved specimen such as myself. *The rose of May.* Why couldn't she tell me first? Instead she runs straight to her father – the doddering old idiot – and he flaps off to my mother, and then all three of them gang up against me behind my back, gloating that now they've really got something they can hold against me. And *she's* the one who put me straight in their trap!'

He finished with an outraged flourish, which nevertheless concealed a new note of insistent anxiety. *Thou wouldst not think how ill all's here about my heart.* I observed that Ophelia would have found it impossible to communicate anything to him about the pregnancy in his present paranoid state. And it was not parental expectations which disturbed him, but hopes and fears of his own. As in the "To be or not to be" dream, what frightened him was the idea of falling in love, entering a state of hopefulness – the possibility that he, too, could be a real lover. All the victims of his present comprehensive attack represented his own love-objects – his mother, Ophelia, myself in the analysis, Shakespeare. These love-objects evoked in him expectations of himself. *John-a-dreams, unpregnant of his cause.*

At this he swore and hit his fist on the edge of the couch, to express his unutterable ridicule and rage. Then he hissed, "Can't you put yourself in my position for once – can't you even see how they're all ganging up to attack *me*?'

I said he was so convinced he was the victim, that it was difficult for him to see that it was something in himself which he was attacking – the internal objects which represented the kind of beauty which was truth. Truthful communication with such an internal object, through his external love-objects, would involve sacrificing his vanity and egoism. He could conceive of trying to control Ophelia, and of Ophelia trying to control him, but not of engaging his development with hers on a level deeper than the possession of physical beauty. This would be to discover the inner beauty or truth of a person, the love-object. He could not conceive that his parents had done this, that Shakespeare had done it with his play, that I did it with psychoanalysis – that this is what is meant by being a lover.

"You're always on the woman's side, aren't you?" he said accusingly, "whatever the facts of the case – they're always right, and I'm always wrong. Can't you put yourself in *my* position for once?"

And what, I asked, were the facts of the case? To what extent was it an accident, and to what extent did he really believe

Ophelia was innocent and he was responsible? For, surprised though I had been by the news of Ophelia's pregnancy, Hamlet's persistent hostility to the event gave me the increasing impression that it was not the accident it had first seemed. *The forehead of an innocent love.*

"The facts", he said irritably and evasively, "are that Ophelia's as old as I am and this is 1974 – are you accusing me of rape or something? Because I can assure you, nothing could be further from the "truth" – as you like to have it. Like all women, she knows precisely what she's doing, and she's been doing it with God knows how many others besides me."

I reminded him of the aristocracy of Athens who had to go to whores to practise sex because they were frightened of impotence. He was acting like one of those aristocrats.

"Why the hell should I believe it was anything to do with me anyway?" he then exploded. "There's nothing to prove it was me. You should hear what Nando says about her – he knows her better than most. And I told you about Rosenfeld – he's a sly swine! What about Forte? He's been after her for ages – he was always snooping about in the wings during the performance – you could see for a fact he was just waiting to grab Ophelia after the show."

This, I said immediately, was his jealousy. Previously, in his princely omnipotence, he had assumed Ophelia was his indisputable possession. Now, it suddenly seemed to him that she was surrounded by men waiting to seize her from the wings. The fact of her pregnancy had jolted him out of his security, his arrogance.

"Jealous! I'm not jealous of Forte!" he sneered. "And you're wrong, I don't think I own her – it's her business. There's no accounting for taste. I don't pretend to be her keeper – I mean, half the nights of the week I'm down here seeing you. I just think she should honestly admit who did it, that's all."

Evidently the pregnancy was something inconceivable to him, an event which could not possibly have been generated by their relationship. He really couldn't believe it had anything to do with him, though I still suspected he had engineered it unconsciously in order to confirm his ownership of Ophelia, but then found himself completely thrown by the reality. Instead of securing his position as the prince, it made him feel yet again that he had been ejected, humiliated – somebody else must have done it behind his back. I pondered on this with interest, and much more sympathy, as his youthful vulnerability (so long obscured by the Mousetrap) presented itself to me with renewed force. My anger evaporated a little as I considered the likely doubts about his own success as a lover which lay behind his new experience of jealousy. His activities as a lover, he felt, seemed to bear no relation to this pregnancy which had struck like a bolt from the blue.

Meanwhile, I wondered, who or what was this Forte who had suddenly appeared within the circle of his intimate acquaintance? *Making mouths at the invisible event.* Whoever he might refer to in actuality, I could see that I was going to have a long and hard struggle with what one might call Hamlet's own "Forte" consciousness. This was his hardening omnipotence – his defence against his new vulnerability. *Exposing what is mortal and unsure, even for an eggshell.*

To the final session before the break, however, he brought a dream which marked a watershed in the analysis. The dream referred to the last performance of his play, which his parents had come to watch. In the dream, *his mother was sitting in the front row watching the play. Then she got up, and began to walk slowly and deliberately up on to the stage where he was. She was wearing long voluminous robes and had a diadem on her forehead. The heavy crimson stage curtains closed behind her, and she spoke reproachfully to Hamlet, saying:*

"*Hamlet, you have greatly offended your father, and he is no longer prepared to play on the same stage with you.*"

Hamlet replied, "*Don't you like this mirror image of your inmost parts?*" *Then he noticed a strange twitching movement low down amongst the folds of her dress, which he found repulsive, and instinctively stabbed at it viciously with a stage dagger – to discover that it was not an animal as he had supposed, but Professor Polack, the size of a dwarf, bowing and grinning. His mother gave a deep sigh and sank to her knees, saying, "Hamlet, you have broken my heart in two." Then the dwarf Professor grew in stature like one of those genii from a magic lamp, and metamorphosed into his father, Claude, who seemed to hover over him. His father was clothed in a familiar loose Japanese-style silk dressing gown with a water-lily pattern, whose sleeves moved as if in a light breeze as he held out his arms towards Hamlet, saying:*

"Remember, Hamlet, taint not thy mind nor harm thy mother."

Hamlet felt beads of sweat on his forehead. He felt he was looking at a ghost. What seemed to terrify him specifically was his father's gaze fixed on him. In fact he begged this new Ghost:

> *"Do not look on me, lest you convert*
> *The blood-red colour of my masculine revenge*
> *Into watery tears and the sort of giving way*
> *That would trouble a woman."*

Then the stage curtains opened again, and Hamlet to his humiliation saw the cartoon-like faces of the audience leering and laughing.

Here was the Mousetrap indeed, and Hamlet's own dream-analysis of the significance of the acting-out of the past many weeks. At last I had some clear evidence to show Hamlet his little-boy vulnerability, as he managed to relinquish the claustrophobic identification with a macho internal father which had been dominating his state of mind.

His difficulty in relating the dream was evident. In sarcastic tones he mimicked a bathetic plaintive voice for his mother and a booming ponderous one for his father. It seemed to be the final humiliation which rankled, rather than the murderous implications of his own actions in the dream.

"I'm sick of being treated like a child!" he fumed. "One minute they pat you on the head and the next they kick you up the arse."

In the dream, it seemed, he was indeed a child, who had intruded into his parents' bedroom (represented by the stage), acting as if he owned the place. Indeed the double layers of drapery (the long dress, the curtains closing behind her) indicated his mother's inmost parts, which he had attacked by stabbing the dwarf-size Professor-baby within her. *That great baby scarce out of his swaddling clothes.* Swaddled in his mother's arras.

"Silly old prick", snapped Hamlet. "The voice of moralism getting its just deserts." *Rash intruding fool.*

I reminded him of how he had been driven out of his little room, the "hamster cage", owing to his claustrophobic sense of being inside his mother, controlling her. This had also been his attitude to Ophelia, directing her in the Mousetrap. Her pregnancy, however, had undermined this role. And now, the linking of his various father-figures to warn him against damaging his internal objects suggested there could be a transforming, reparative power at work, very different from the punitive "revenge" of a disciplinarian father, or the disordered thinking of a word-twisting father.

"You mean, it's as though they're all ganging up against me", was Hamlet's paranoid response. "I don't need a ghost in a dream to tell me that." *There needs no ghost from the grave to tell us this.*

It was, I said, his own continual splitting which was being confronted by the dream – like his mother saying her heart was "split in two". *Live the purer with the other half.*

"That's your interpretation, anyway", he muttered. "From my point of view it would be a good thing if she learned to make distinctions."

He didn't like to think the idealized fighter-pilot, the sensual diplomat-businessman, the guardian of literature, and myself as the protector of psychoanalysis, could all be aspects of the same internal father-figure.

"Oh come on!" he sneered. "You put stuff like that in your scientific papers, so-called. Yet you object to poetic ambiguities in my interpretation of a play."

It was the dream itself that disturbed him, I said, not my interpretation of it – the emotional facts were there in front of us.

For my part I was disturbed by his present instability, and emphasized to him the warning of violence contained in the dream, and the aggressive feelings aroused by Ophelia's pregnancy. It was impossible to tell what form his vulnerability and sense of humiliation might take during the two-week break in analysis. *He that is mad and sent to England.* Nevertheless the dream was clearly a turning-point in terms of Hamlet's release from his claustrophobic identification with his father's overtly military hero-penis. This marked the beginning of the end of his delusory uncle-father. I pointed out the reparative direction indicated by the new Ghost-father when he said that revenge on womanly feelings could be converted into tears. On this tenuous contact I had to base my hopes that he would survive the Christmas break without erupting or collapsing.

CHAPTER FIVE

The Grave

> **Hamlet**: Witness this army of such mass and charge,
> Led by a delicate and tender prince,
> Whose spirit, with divine ambition puff'd,
> Makes mouths at the invisible event,
> Exposing what is mortal and unsure
> To all that fortune, death, and danger dare,
> Even for an eggshell. (IV. iv. 47-53)

Horacio unearths the anxieties behind the question of Ophelia's abortion and Hamlet's relation with the Forte family, and is rewarded by the Grave dream and Hamlet's new dependence.

The Monday after the Christmas break, Hamlet was delivered to the door in an MG sports car, twenty minutes late for the early morning session. He stumbled uncertainly down the steps and entered the consulting room looking uncharacteristically dirty and dishevelled, his clothes smelling strongly of stale tobacco smoke and marijuana. *High and mighty, I am set naked on your kingdom.*

"Sorry I'm late old man", he began; "couldn't make it any earlier. If it hadn't been for Forte I wouldn't have made it at all. The fact is, I don't feel too brill. I know what you're thinking - you're surprised at me having anything to do with him, seeing he's such a pansy joker. Well – it's sheer coincidence. He just gave me a lift, that's all – on the way to his office. I had a long way to come. He's cool enough in his way – got an MG. Coupé. The fact is, I had the most awful dream last night – or the night before. We were all at this groovy affair at Forte's place in the country – his mother's place that is. Bedfordshire. Some of us are still there. *A convocation of politic worms.* Amazing."

It was the first time I had seen Hamlet befuddled through drink or drugs (of which he was normally very contemptuous, claiming he didn't need to indulge in such stuff, and satirizing the "moronic glazed" attitudes of his friends when "stoned"). *Thieves of mercy.* But I wondered if this was all that lay behind his disjointed attention, and inquired after the dream he had mentioned.

"Yeah, that was pretty awful ..." he drawled. "They've got a house right out in the country in the middle of nowhere, with a huge barn, where everybody could doss down together. You could really freak out – there was live music all night – two groups, lights, a proper bar. All professional stuff, nothing tatty or amateur." *Tomb and continent enough to hide the slain.*

I pointed out he had been so impressed by the facilities at this party that he had failed to keep his commitment to me.

"Look man, I said I was sorry, didn't I?" he said more energetically, recovering his powers of speech. "I knew you'd be ratty, but it couldn't be helped. Everybody was there, everybody. Weird really, I always thought Forte was poncy and stuck-up, but now I reckon he's just shy. And lonely. He's an only child, like me – but spoilt to death. He's always had everything he wants – this was his twenty-first birthday party. His people are pretty interesting too. His father is away most of the time, he does documentaries and things. *Old Norway, impotent and bedrid, scarce sees his son.* But his mother is amazing, really way out, I've never come across a woman like her, with such a powerful personality. She writes articles on progressive culture – you know – self-awareness, alternative society and stuff. She's owner and also Lifestyle Editor for *The Dictator*" (he said impressively). "So it's her business to see what's coming before anyone else does. It's odd because Forte is such a traditional type; if they still had bowler hats he'd be wearing one – he's a born-again conservative. Yeah", Hamlet added in complacent tones, "I'm more sympathetic to him now. I can see his problems. I bet Mrs F even organized the party for him, to help him break the ice. Yeah, that's how it was. I see it now."

I pointed out to Hamlet the resemblance between himself and Forte in his description. Here again we were confronted with the lonely, only child in him, "spoilt to death" and unhappy with his parents. *I lack advancement.* There also seemed to be expressed his revulsion at his mother's society parties, and her own fashionable but dilettante, and possibly controlling, cultural patronage. A question was forming at the back of my mind about the impact of the family culture on Hamlet – was there really something rotten in the house of Denmark? I asked Hamlet if he thought Forte's problems included his mother and her "powerful personality". *A portentous figure.*

"God no", he responded in astonishment. "She's not shocked by anything – not like my mother. It could be she's a bit heavy for Forte, of course, a bit too dynamic. No, I had a really serious conversation with her. I've got an idea she wants to write an article about me – she saw my play at Christmas - said she could see straight away I was going places. 'Art must come first', she said, and I said that's just what I said! I told her it was bugging me that my talent might get diluted by hereditary considerations, and how I needed to get the status quo off my back – funny thing is –"

I interrupted to ask Hamlet to define more precisely the difference between Mrs Forte and his own mother. "Well for a start you can really talk to her", he explained confidentially. "I told her all about my problems with Ophelia and she said she could help – she knows a good clinic, a new one, none of this filthy backstreet stuff that's still hanging on, and it would all be over in ten minutes. Oh yeah – and the funny thing was, she knew an amazing amount about psychoanalysis. She was really well informed. I'm sure she must have tried it herself, at least she's read all about it. She knew I was in analysis of course, and said it was a wonderful opportunity for self-observation. I said yes it was, just way out. It's amazing what you can see when you really look. 'Sit here', she said, sinking into a pile of cushions with her joint, 'sit here and tell me all about it. First of all, what school are you under?' And you won't believe it, Dr Horacio, but my tongue completely seized up. I was fazed, I felt completely gormless. *Unpregnant of my cause, I could say nothing.* It's never happened to me before. I thought, she'll think I'm a complete phoney, a freak. I know what you're going to say – what can I expect if I get stoned out of my mind? But she was very understanding – said we'd carry on our talk another time, because she could see I was no tame talent, I was really screwed up and obscure ..."

I was disturbed at the extent to which Hamlet had evidently felt intimidated by this predatory mother-of-Grendel figure, and at the same time flattered by her seductive attentions. Certainly she seemed to represent a caricature of his mother with her patronage of young artists – the iron lady rather than the sick soul. I could sense, through Hamlet, how flattering it did indeed appear. What disturbed me as Hamlet gave his account was the possibility that this woman could seriously interfere with the analysis. If Hamlet became her protégé she could choose to either patronize or surreptitiously attack him or indeed myself through the media – my work, my private life. Such journalistic assaults by professional snoopers were not uncommon in the field. It was well known that those who had "tried" analysis, and been unable to discover any capacity for passionate experience, became either enemies or apostles of psychoanalysis; and it was hard to tell which was the more damaging.

Hamlet had told Mrs Forte "all about" Ophelia. This was unfortunate. I was relieved, for the time being, when he then described how he had been unable to say a word about me or the analysis. I suggested to Hamlet that his tongue had "seized up" as a means of protecting areas which he wanted to keep private. There was a discrepancy between this and saying he could really talk to her.

"It was because I was stoned", he insisted sulkily. *Am I pigeon-livered, lacking gall?* "You wouldn't know. I mean it's not my scene at all, I'm not habituated. You're such an old romantic with your fancy theories. Anyway I *could* talk – I told her about Ophelia, didn't I? And she understood perfectly – not like my mother."

Clearly he was not sufficiently aware of the intentions behind Mrs Forte's seductions to be on his guard. My anxiety increased, and I asked him who he believed to be more sincerely concerned for his and Ophelia's welfare – his mother or this woman. He mumbled crossly that it was a stupid question: Mrs Forte didn't know Ophelia, she wasn't at the party – but that made her advice more genuine and impartial. The whole set-up was different. She didn't have designs on him like his own family. I pointed out that not only had he suspected her of "designing" the entire party, such that the professionalism of the occasion made him feel he and his friends were being used, rather than entertained, for the satisfaction of Mrs Forte's own "trendy" ambitions; but also, Hamlet had clearly experienced her interrogation as that of a witch-like figure who wanted to squeeze from him his deepest and dirtiest secrets, "screwed up and obscure". Moreover, his tongue seizing up suggested he felt he had in some way betrayed Ophelia to outside interference – that it was in fact none of Mrs Forte's business. His feelings of guilt about Ophelia made him vulnerable to this sort of interference.

"Why shouldn't I get advice from an older woman?" he snapped, increasingly irritated. "It seems to me that was just the right thing to do. And she does at least live in the real world of today. My mother inhabits a different planet – some Parisian salon from the last century."

The "different planet", I said, was the field of intimate relationships, such as he was engaged with through his own family or the Polack family. Different values pertained to these from those in the world of non-intimate relationships - fashion, status, power etcetera – as represented here by his picture of Mrs Forte and possibly the whole Forte "set-up" as it had impressed itself on Hamlet.

"At least, in the Forte set-up, I didn't feel like something the dog brought in", he said in self-justificatory growl. "It makes a change to feel *welcome* somewhere."

He had, I suggested, been looking for an alternative analyst to me, a seductive substitute for mental pain. It was here in the consulting room, in the context of his intimate inner world, that he felt unwelcome.

"Well yeah" he flashed, "it's true I was getting sick of being abused and moralized at by you the whole time!"

He was the lonely Forte-child, I said, and I was the Mrs Forte witch-mummy who was trying to abuse his talents for my own ends. The fact that Mrs Forte was a woman, who perhaps ought to "welcome" feelings, care about his girlfriend or himself, seemed to have particularly intimidated him. Indeed, he had seemed to find his own attack on feminine or intimate values reflected in her, making him prey to her seductions – a species of emotional blackmail. *There is no alternative, the iron lady always said.* But, as his tongue "seizing up" had showed, he had also, in another part of himself, interpreted her interest as being essentially anti-analytic, and had used this means to preserve his intimacy. But he still regarded this episode of word-failure in the light of a humiliation. "What are you, some kind of a sadist?" he scowled. "Or is it just your obsession with digging up material for your scientific papers? It's really you not Mrs Forte who can't resist displaying your theories in journalese. Just remember, whatever you write, maybe it's *you* who's inventing the whole thing!"

He slouched off in a prickly, ugly mood, quite different from the dozy benevolence of his arrival. He never did tell the "awful" dream he mentioned at the beginning, and I suspected it only existed in the form of the interrogation by Mrs Forte. As I went next door to soothe myself with a cigarette, I reflected on my own peculiar agitation during this session. His tongue seizing up had been in a sense a manifestation of his faith in me and the analysis. Yet the more I had insisted on this, the more ground I felt I was losing to the enemy. Was that the problem – the enemy? Had I attacked Mrs Forte too personally, rather than interpreting her significance in the transference? Certainly I had felt a strong personal antagonism to this woman I didn't even know. Was this because she seemed to represent for me, as for Hamlet, certain aspects of his mother which I could not bear to believe were really part of her character? I must, I thought, get a better hold of myself and my technique in this sensitive situation.

And, during the next session, I had to struggle hard to submit to my own warning. Hamlet arrived swollen with sanctimonious elation, and announced that he had had a bitter row with Ophelia over the question of an abortion.

"She's got the same obstinacy as her brother but obviously hasn't got even his wits – and they're spread thin enough. *The mortality of a young maid's wits.* I explained everything to her - as long as she gets on with it now, it's quick, it's easy, it's painless. The more she fools around pulling silly faces the worse it's going to be. It's crazy. I've found out everything about it – this place where it's all absolutely above board, everything is clean and respectable, no questions asked – in fact nobody need even know. Who doesn't already that is. *That*, of course, is half our problem: instead of telling me straight in the first place, so we could sort it out honestly together, she's gone blurting it out to the world and his wife – her old fool of a father, my besotted mother, the lot. And Nando, of course – he knows too." *Let the doors be shut on them all.*

Perhaps, I suggested, Ophelia did not require "explaining to" but questioning about her own feelings. We could see from Hamlet's tyrannical language that he was back in the Mousetrap mentality again. Now, he was behaving as though Ophelia and their parents were ganging up to mousetrap *him*. This was the paranoid consequence of his own attack on his parents in the play, which involved holding Ophelia up to ridicule. Now it seemed to him that, through this pregnancy, she was taking revenge on him and on his adaptation of Shakespeare.

"Well it's screwing *her* up as much as me", he continued, with unabated dogmatism. "The fact is, I need to get this sorted out once and for all so it doesn't keep getting in the way of our relationship. I said to her – let's look at this rationally – does she really *want* to have the bloody thing? Be tied down for the rest of her life, say goodbye to her musical career – because if she drops out now, she'll never make it, she'll be a leftover. And when I asked her straight out, do you want to have it, she said she 'didn't know'! So there you are – it's not even as though she wanted it, she can see quite well it would be lunatic."

Hamlet's was speaking with extraordinary speed and excitability. *Unpacking his heart with words.* I found I was interrupting him as much to slow him down as to get him to listen. What, I asked, was the "it" that was "screwing Ophelia up" – was it the pregnancy, or was it perhaps him? In a manner familiar to us, he had interpreted Ophelia's "don't know" answer in terms of his own assumptions. He was looking for proof that she didn't want it, not for evidence of her feelings; nor had he taken account of his own bullying tone and the distorting effect this might have on her answer.

"I just told her the honest truth! If it isn't dealt with now, we'll all pay for it later – can you deny that?"

What was his honest intention, I asked - did he sincerely wish to discover what Ophelia's feelings were, or was his "honesty" really intended to prevent himself from finding out?

"Perhaps you should have *her* in analysis if you're so keen to find out", he hissed sarcastically; "you won't believe what *I* say." Then with a self-righteous air, as if controlling his justifiable rage: "All right, if you really want to know, I'll tell you precisely, in plain terms, how it was. After I'd explained everything, she went very quiet, and gave me some peculiar looks. She was obviously considering my argument carefully, because she didn't disagree in any way (how could she anyway? the facts are plain). I told her I wanted her to know that in spite of all this pregnancy thing, I was still really keen on her. The last thing we wanted was to wreck our relationship at this point. And I appreciated she could do with some time on her own, to take it all in, so after that I left her – I didn't want to be insensitive. The thing is, when she quietened down and just sat there looking at me, I realized how fond I was of her, and I told her I just couldn't wait for us to shove this big shadow out the way so we could get back together again. Then she smiled, and looked almost like the old Ophelia. I promised I'd see her today so we could fix it up. So, in the circumstances", concluded Hamlet with a crazy triumph, "I've done everything I possibly could. Especially when you consider that the brat probably isn't mine anyway – I'm just the one to take responsibility."

Yes, I thought, focussing on his last remark – that was at the root of his entrenched mania. Confirmation was growing for this predominant anxiety. This was his "big shadow". *The illness about his heart.* I asked him for his evidence for suspecting the child was not his.

"Evidence!" he laughed scornfully. "I can tell you she wasn't a virgin when I first had her – and it was easy enough to get her into bed. That throws it all in doubt. *Puzzles the will.* Do you want to know the evidence for that too? Or am I supposed to call up witnesses? What can I do to satisfy your scientific Honour?"

I reminded him of the early stages of his relationship with Ophelia – the Batman dream of sweeping her off her feet, the "fuck, fuck" poem which was really his own romantic vision of opening her "ventages" to a new and blissful world of erotic experience. Clearly his discovery that she was not a virgin had undermined his romantic role as he had conceived it. His anxiety was, that instead of being the first to awaken her desire, she had gone to bed with him easily out of habit, an easy lay – the secret whore of his phantasy. Not being a virgin also meant that she was in a position to compare his performance with that of other men. *Remembrances to redeliver.* Doubts about his own success as a lover then aroused suspicions that she had continued to have other lovers.

This suggestion enraged him further. "What's it to me if she did or didn't?" he cried. "It's beneath my dignity to interrogate her – like you would if you had the chance."

I told him he was not prepared to be compared with anyone else; it was an assumption of his princely mentality that with his genius and attributes, he was simply not in the same league as other men – he was incomparable.

"Is it too much to expect straightforward honesty from a woman? Do I have to have suspicions and grub about in the dirt just so I can satisfy you with some cheap romantic slurp?"

His own romantic view of Ophelia's virginity had led him to another type of dishonesty, I said – the dishonesty of not expressing his doubts to Ophelia. Had he considered her position, deprived of any chance to understand his hostility? *Rich gifts wax poor when givers prove unkind.*

"Ophelia, Ophelia!" he interjected scathingly. "You seem mighty concerned about Ophelia. How d'you think *I* feel, with all this hanging over me?"

I said I thought he felt let down by this pregnancy, no longer in control of events and of Ophelia in particular. The directorial "fuck fuck" side of himself had been undermined by something which suddenly brought into focus all his doubts about Ophelia's appreciation of him as a lover, and about the quality of her love for him. These were linked in his mind with his doubts about the parentage of the baby. Yet instead of discussing this with her, he had merely harangued and bullied her, just as he had his mother earlier. *Wouldst thou be a breeder of sinners?* In effect he was demanding that she get rid of the baby to prove she belonged only to him, just as he had demanded that Gertrude must get rid of the usurper Claude.

"So what are you really saying?" he snapped sarcastically, "that she ought to have it after all? And then, I suppose, we'll live Happy Ever After. For God's sake, Dr Horacio – get real. How could a couple at our stage in life make it lumbered with a baby – isn't it time you stopped tilting at windmills?"

Neither of them, I insisted, had even set out on the road at the end of which a decision might be possible. They had not begun to consider what it "meant" to each of them to have the baby aborted, or as Hamlet put it to "shove this big shadow out of the way". I reminded him of his recent Mousetrap dream with its clear expression of taking revenge by killing the baby inside the mother. There was the sincere or truthful meaning of his wanting Ophelia to have the abortion. It occurred to me here that that dream probably also expressed his own fear that somehow he had caused his mother to have abortions in the past, leaving him an only child like Forte.

"Oh come on", he said contemptuously. "The reality of this bloody abortion is that it's not a baby at this stage, just a blob of cells. The important thing is, to do it quickly." *Be it thought and done.*

The mantra of Macbeth, I reminded him. This emphasis on precipitate action – "doing it quickly" – was, as he well knew, aimed at preventing thinking from taking place. He used the word "reality" as if it were the explanation to end all questions. Our concern was to identify the emotional reality, not the biological reality. We already had evidence of his tendency to split Ophelia into outside and inside, upper and lower parts, as his means of convincing himself that he controlled her movements and her meaning. This omnipotent attitude of his had been challenged by the pregnancy, and therefore, I believed, a new and uncontrollable jealousy had been awoken in him.

Hamlet received this renewed interpretation of jealousy with snorts of unutterable contempt, and left at the end of the session more defiant and sanctimonious than ever. I was the one who would suffer (he implied) from my own perversity in not accepting his honest explanations of the best course of action, and my persistence in an oldfashioned romantic viewpoint.

He was mildly surprised when (as he reported at the next session) Ophelia told him to "sod off" - their relationship was over and she would never speak to him again. But it failed utterly to dent his mania. He said it merely confirmed his suspicion that the "real" father was "Forte or somebody" after all, and he'd been a fool to be so willing to assume responsibility. If she wanted to blame the right man, that was OK by him. He'd done his duty.

"She had a nerve taking that self-righteous tone with me", he concluded. "It could have been Nando for all I know – he's been screwing her for years and that's a fact – so why not?"

Probably, I suggested, he was making this assumption as a result of his own earlier homosexual relationship with Nando. Had he asked himself for any actual evidence for this "fact" as he called it?

He gave a coarse, barking laugh and said it was "obvious – what do you think brothers and sisters do together? If I'd had a sister to practise on I'd have done the same."

"Obvious", I repeated – there he went again!

"Yes, obvious, obvious!" he almost shouted. *Cursing like a very drab*. And so it went on. By the end of the session my hand was itching with the impulse to clout him. So when I stood up as he left, after opening the door, I kept my arms pinioned firmly to my sides. He noticed this.

"Krup-ke!" he said in a military bark, raising his fingers in an ambiguous salute, before slithering round the corner.

I was left troubled, and puzzled, by my inability to make any headway with him, or to bring him in touch with his own emotional state. Again I felt I had somehow lost credibility with him through engaging in partisan debate. Despite support from the evidence of his previous dreams, the transference had again become obscured by what he saw as my moral preaching - my hostility to his tyranny, my urgency that he should repair his relationship with Ophelia. My own desire, as he had seen, was that they should have the baby; did this, perhaps, colour all my interpretations? If so, it might explain why he had seemed impervious to them. I was Krupke again, the authoritarian (and rather stupid) moralizer – no longer the analyst.

For two weeks we continued in this situation of deadlock. Meanwhile I reviewed the last sessions, and the entire Mousetrap episode, in my mind, and bit by bit I structured the situation for him. We went over the attack on his mother in the Mousetrap dream; and his princely attitude to Ophelia in the Batman dream and how he regarded her as his possession. He had deviously engineered the pregnancy as proof of this, and likewise was trying to engineer the abortion as a test of her love for him. She must prove her willingness to abandon everything else for his sake. But his plans had backfired: the event of the pregnancy had come instead to seem like Ophelia's revenge on him, having awoken hidden doubts and fears about her love for him, and his stature as a lover in her eyes, particularly as she was resisting his demands for an abortion. Hence the ugliness of his behaviour toward her. And, I explained to Hamlet, all this derived from his own infantile competitiveness with his creative internal parents – with aspects of Polack, Claude, Gertrude, Shakespeare – and above all with myself in the transference as his analytic father. This first became evident in the Mousetrap, which was intended to rival the genius of Shakespeare, but in fact, as he only realized afterwards, merely held up to ridicule the woman he loved. It resulted directly in the pregnancy, another effort to secure her by a display of all-powerful creativity, which had also failed. The demand for an abortion was his next attempt in the same line.

As the complete pattern of this manic episode of acting-out unfolded itself in all its inevitability, with its increasing focus on the analysis as a creative process envied and attacked by his little-boy rivalry, Hamlet's wild fury and accusations gradually gave way to periods of quiet and gloomy depression. I began to feel that I was slowly but steadily regaining some of the ground lost by my own exciteability over the Mousetrap. Then one day Hamlet arrived looking altered, pale and slightly shaken. He had had a dream which he compared to a childish nightmare, though at the time it had not seemed childish but deadly serious.

In the dream *he was walking along a high coastal path, such as he knew from childhood holidays in the West Country, when he suddenly had the intimation that he was being followed, by a wild beast which he knew to be a bear. The terrifying thing was that the bear's long shadow was in advance of it, so that Hamlet found himself walking and then running in the shadow.*

> *As who, pursued with yell and blow,*
> *Still treads the shadow of his foe.*

He felt impelled to glance backwards to see if the bear was nearly upon him, and at that moment fell into a deep hole like a well, landing flat on his back. He realized then, as he looked upwards, that the well was a newly dug grave;

> *and I*
> *Was lying on a bed of bones, my mouth*
> *Bunged chokingly with dirt. Equivocation*
> *Was undoing me. In panic I flung*
> *The bones in handfuls upwards, but they showered*
> *Down again and hit me about the head.*
> *In revulsion I wept, and through my tears*
> *Noticed in the corner of the grave*
> *A skull that grew fresh lips, inviting me*
> *To climb on its back and play. My gorge rose,*
> *Abhorring this lady's chamber,*

> *Its gibes, its gambols, its flashes of merriment.*
> *Like a genie from a lamp, an old woman*
> *Grew from the skull and set me gently*
> *Down on the turf at the grave's brink. The waters*
> *Rose below me, and there I saw floating*
> *Ophelia, garlanded with flowers, her clothes*
> *Spread wide in the aqueous element, and drinking*
> *Greedily its moisture. Growing heavier*
> *She sang a mermaid's song, like one*
> *Natively endowed with that condition.*

I was astounded by the unanticipated depth of feeling "welling up" out of this "Grave dream", which for so many weeks Hamlet had prevented from breaking through. *Tears shall be your recreation.* Here was the "big shadow" of the threatened baby (as Hamlet had earlier described it), taking the vengeful bear-shape which caused Hamlet to "fall" out of his impenetrable omnipotence into a "grave" condition. There was even, in the dream, a clear indication that this could be the site of his repentance and "recreation" through tears.

I was intrigued by the "funny old woman"; Hamlet said she reminded him of those disguised "good fairies" in fairy-tales. *A fellow of infinite jest.* I agreed she seemed to be, as it were, the opposite number to the Mrs Forte-witch who presided over abortions; and that the dream generally showed a greater appreciation of the impact of femininity than we had seen before in his dreams. For the first time, we had a clear glimpse of Hamlet's maternal transference to me in the analysis, his baby-like dependence. It was an encouraging development – quite different in quality from his initial automatic dependence on me, which derived from the prince in him lacking a confidante.

The session after this, however, Hamlet came in with the news that Ophelia had had an abortion. He had spent the previous night at the house which Nando shared with Forte and others in Islington, in order to avoid seeing his parents when he came down from Cambridge for his appointments with me. Nando had told him that Ophelia was "no longer pregnant, so he needn't worry about that any more". To his surprise, this news filled Hamlet with an explosive fury, and he demanded to "thrash" Nando at a game of squash. *Woo't weep? Woo't fight? Woo't tear thyself?* They went out and played for two hours, during which Hamlet was thoroughly beaten by Nando (by far the better player). He said that the game had greatly relieved him.

Hamlet had not, in fact, seen Ophelia since the crazy interview he had recounted to me. She was not well, he said in low and guilt-ridden tones, and was staying at home. He knew that she truly hated him. He didn't need to ask anyone that, he could sense it; besides she had told him as much. But now, he had a new goal in life, which was to beat Nando at squash, and he had arranged to play with him on a regular basis. *To outface him by leaping in her grave.*

CHAPTER SIX

The Winter's Tale

> **Queen**: Her clothes spread wide,
> And mermaid-like awhile they bore her up,
> Which time she chanted snatches of old lauds,
> As one incapable of her own distress,
> Or like a creature native and indued
> Unto that element. (IV. vii. 174-179)

Still Horacio does not see the depth of Hamlet's despair during the following period of persecutory depression and guilt. The Winter's Tale dream, together with Ophelia's recovery, encourages a false hope of his own.

By the time he learned of Ophelia's abortion and illness, Hamlet's demeanour had already commenced its sea-change from the Mousetrap mania. He became subdued and depressed, and this depression, in the context of the analytic work, had produced the fascinating Grave dream. After this, he was often silent for long periods during sessions, and for many weeks oscillated between withdrawal, depression and paranoia. He made decided efforts to co-operate in the analysis, coming on time to the sessions and bringing whatever he could remember in the way of dreams. These were invariably repetitive "grave dreams" on the lines of his being imprisoned in the dark somewhere with only small windows for eyes on the world, despairing of release. *Loopholes onto the stage of the world.* None of these dreams had the emotional depth of the original Grave dream. There was, however, a new element which linked back to that dream and his falling into the grave – it was his strong identification with the aborted baby. He experienced himself as having similarly been flung into the rectum, discarded, to await evacuation.

Hamlet was not under the tutorship of Professor Polack this term. I gathered he was doing very little work, and he seemed to have given up most of his extra-curricular activities, apart from a fanatical adherence to playing squash with Nando whenever he was in London. This was the only area in which he manifest any spark of vitality. It meant that when he came to his sessions he had usually either played or was about to play squash. It was his ambition, he said, to become good enough to beat Nando at the game. *Frankly play this brothers' wager.*

"Nando belongs to a private sports club with fabulous facilities. And actually, he's a bloody good teacher in his way. One of these days I shall really beat the hell out of him. That's why I've taken up meat-eating again. I need to build myself up. Anyway everybody's going vegetarian these days, it's just a fad with them not a principle."

He saw fighting Nando as a means of both punishing and rebuilding himself. Frequently, over the next month or two, I tried to explain to him that it was also a way of avoiding confronting his feelings. He was out of touch with his vengeful jealousy of Nando (who represented Ophelia's lover, in his eyes), which was his real motive for fighting him. Above all, he was out of touch with his anxiety that he had intruded on Ophelia, killing her baby.

The news he gave about Ophelia was not good. She had officially taken leave of absence from her studies, because she was suffering from severe depression and had twice tried to slit her wrists. Afraid of leaving her alone at all, her father had arranged for her to spend a period in hospital, where she was in a ward amongst (mainly) anorexic girls.

"Nando says being in with that lot would drive anyone off their rocker even if they weren't crazy before", said Hamlet grimly. "He says the only advantage is, she can't slit her wrists. He makes it sound like some kind of a joke, but underneath I know he thinks I'm a real shit." He spoke in a flat, dull tone, as though he were religiously making himself report the entire unsavoury truth; and proceeded, putting his sentences together with an effort:

"I can never face Polly again either. It's his own stupid fault. Why did he have to get so idiotically excited over any old trashy thing I'd written? He was even disappointed when I gave up writing for that obsolete rag *Varsity*. He expected me to leap through the hoops like a performing monkey to boost his own fading ego. Same as Claude – just to make me feel guilty. Why should I be his instrument, or anybody's? And now they've landed me in this mess."

Hamlet's tone was one of gloomy complaint. Clearly he was somehow blaming Professor Polack's attitude to his work for stimulating a false excitement, a showing-off, in his own relation to Ophelia. I did wonder if he had felt he was unable to live up to Polack's expectations (which seemed to have been a little idealized), rather as he had turned against his father. *Th'expectancy and rose of the fair state.* Though it looked as though this idealization had bored rather than daunted him. In some way it had damped his interest, in the tutor and possibly in the subject. Hamlet agreed with this:

"It was his fault for making me into something I wasn't. It just showed how out of touch he was, like Claude – a complete dinosaur. As if I was something out of Pseuds Corner."

Now the pressure of his claustrophobic identification with his "uncle-father" had been relieved, I said, he was plunged into a persecutory depression. He felt a pseud, a dinosaur, ridiculous – stimulated and encouraged by these fathers only to be laughed at afterwards for being merely a little boy. *A pipe for Fortune's finger.* His own sexual activity seemed unrelated to the possibility of his ever joining the ranks of true fatherhood.

"What you mean is", he said moodily, "I'm a lousy, degenerate, inconsiderate slob. You can say it. Can I help it if that is my nature?"

Here, as repeatedly during this period, he sought reassurance from me that I, at least, could see his better nature – that he was only the victim of himself. But his self-blame and self-denigration, I explained, was not the same thing as taking responsibility for his own feelings and actions. This was where our problem lay - in convincing him of the value of feelings, his own and other people's.

"What is it you want me to do, then?" he countered in a more irritable tone. "Grovel in front of them all – shave my head and put on a hair shirt, sleep on a bed of nails? Next you'll be saying I'm disappointing *your* expectations, like the rest of them. Well perhaps my talents just aren't up to it after all."

Again, I repeated gently, it was not a case of doing but of feeling. I suggested that the expectations he was afraid he could never fulfil were not those of winning (action), as when he played squash with Nando, but of emotional communication. He seemed aware that in this area he had a lack of talent. And we could see that his sense of disappointing his father and Polack was now devolving upon me: that I was the one he felt he'd really disappointed.

"Well wasn't it you who was egging me on over the whole business with Ophelia?" he turned on me accusingly, at last. "You can't deny, you were keen to have us married off as soon as possible – is it any wonder I took the shortest road? And you could see all along I was going to make a fool of myself over the play but you never did anything to stop me, did you?"

I said he felt I had not been firm enough to protect him, to contain his little-boy destructive mania. Owing to my weakness, he felt, he had become vulnerable to destructive aspects of himself. The play, the baby, the abortion, now plunged him into the depths of worthlessness; he had crashed. This had been anticipated up to a point in the "To be or not to be" dream. It was not an accident, but the inevitable conclusion to acting-out. Yet it still seemed to be his sense of humiliation – making a fool of himself – that was paramount. And now, he was searching for solutions in the form of action – looking for something to do with his talents – to set this right.

"But as far as the pregnancy goes, I'm still not sure it *was* me – even now", he complained.

I reminded him of how the emotional reality was a separate issue from the genetic paternity, as we'd discussed before. It was what he felt he had done to Ophelia and others in his mind, that meant he couldn't face them.

"You mean, I'm to blame whether it was me or not", he said quickly, with a hint of the old paranoia.

No, I said, I meant that his feelings of guilt were proportional to the damage which he really felt he had caused. And I reviewed with him once again how he felt his sexual relation with Ophelia had begun badly, intrusively, as in the Batman dream and his "fuck fuck" poem; how she had perhaps not felt his "governing her ventages" to be the blissful experience he had expected; how her pregnancy had therefore seemed to be none of his doing; and how her abortion had confirmed his suspicion of his own worthlessness. *An arrant knave crawling between earth and heaven.* Hence in the Grave dream, the bear-baby had turned in revenge and chased him into the grave of deep depression where he was now. This was the emotional reality in his mind, and this was what he had difficulty in facing.

"So what am I supposed to do?", he said with a tinge of repulsion. "Say I didn't mean it, shall we have another go? with my unsuitable genes? I mean, if it *was* mine, she obviously thought it wasn't worth having, didn't she."

I told him he was feeling identified with the baby – thrown out for being worthless. He had wanted Ophelia first to get pregnant, then to have the abortion, to prove she belonged to him. But instead, he felt he had become the victim of her revenge – that she had turned and aborted *him*. It was not unsuitable genes that troubled him, but the painful feeling that he was an intruder who had been discovered masquerading as a provider of babies, and thrown out.

He was silent for a few minutes, then resumed his complaint in pained tones: "What I can't understand", he said, "was how she did it – arranged it, I mean. I can't believe Polly had anything to do with it. That means it must have been Nando, the supercilious slob – or Nando and Forte between them. Which is proof the thing wasn't inseminated by me." He added, with a revived bitterness, "I expect he's laughing at me even now. But I've been practising at Cambridge too, and when I see him tonight I'll really murder him!" *With eyes like carbuncles.*

It was hard, indeed, to convince Hamlet that ultimately there was no substitute for the reality of feeling. A very delicate balance existed throughout this period between his gradual, tentative approach to painful feelings in the analysis, and his belief that action would do instead of confronting the feelings, as in the squash-playing. I reminded him of how he had said Nando had used his sister for practising sex; now, he was practising squash as if this could provide the solution to a painful and confusing emotional problem.

Then, in a new tone of genuine perplexity, he said: "Did she agree to do it to spite me – to show me how worthless I am? Or did she let herself be bullied by those buggers? I just can't understand her!"

I said his not understanding, which he had now repeated twice, was an achievement in itself. Before, he had just regarded Ophelia as an instrument in his own show; now, he spoke as though her motives were not as obvious as her attributes. Perhaps, like the baby which had also been unreal to him, she had something inside her which he accepted was not known by him – her own heart of mystery.

"But you're forgetting", he explained, "I *did* know about her, that was the whole point – I knew her from a little girl, and her family, her music and everything. I knew exactly who she was from the beginning."

But this knowing about, I said, was of course quite different from knowing her intimately in depth – her feelings, motives, desires. We had discussed before his frustration at discovering that sexual relations did not somehow explain everything after all.

He paused for a few moments, ruminating; then began to recount what he had never told me before – his first proper meeting with Ophelia. "The funny thing was", he began, "she was around all the first year of course, and I knew who she was, but I never really noticed her. Even at Polly's, she was always hidden away in a corner, with a friend or something - you never saw her on her own. Then one evening, I bumped into her coming out of the laundrette at the bottom of the hill near Kettle's Yard. She had a plastic bag of laundry in each hand; she reminded me of those French paintings of milkmaids. I had a pile of dirty jumpers in my arms because I'd been told this place still had a dry-cleaning machine. I'd never been there before. She recognized me as she came out and said, "You should wash those by hand, Hamlet", and gave me a very strange smile, almost slightly mocking. It was the first time she'd called me by my name, all the time I'd been in Cambridge, or even really spoken to me. Then she put a bag on each handlebar and wobbled off up the hill back to college. I watched her till she got to the top, all the time thinking to myself, what did she mean? What did she really mean?" *There is much music, excellent voice in this little organ.*

I was interested to hear this description of a more enigmatic, Mona-Lisa like Ophelia in Hamlet's eyes, who had surprised him by not appearing "mouse-like", and who aroused his curiosity rather than his omnipotence. There was also a hint of his often-denied romanticism in the "milkmaid" image. *The rose of May.* It was a view of Ophelia which seemed to have been buried by the Mousetrap affair, or possibly one which had only occurred to Hamlet in retrospect, in the sense of imaginative memory rather than mechanical recall. The self-questioning was definitely a hopeful sign, possibly a way out of his present impasse. I began to feel we were back on firm analytic ground. Perhaps, I suggested to him, we could see here a first step towards his questioning his own sincerity and examining where his own personal worth really lay, rather than pessimistically condemning himself as "worthless" as though this were an inevitable feature of his genetic makeup.

But he responded gloomily that all this was a "pointless exercise. You can't bring back love – that's gone. All that's left is a sort of detached feeling, scientific. Diagnosing the cause of death." *The fall of a sparrow.*

And so it went on in the analysis for many weeks, with Hamlet showing no interest in making any inquiries about why Ophelia had had the abortion, and correspondingly maintaining his own static position in the grave of dead relationships, where nothing was expected from him in terms of communication. It was hard work trying to awaken his capacity to look back and question his own motives and sincerity in the past – all was "pointless" and "hopeless". He preferred to wrap himself in pessimism. The grave was the only secure and comfortable situation to be in, and of course he was reluctant to be disturbed. At the same time I was impressed by his new dependence on me, and by the development of the transference. Elements of both his father and Polack were now regularly gathered into me, and his struggle with them – especially his sense that he had disappointed them – became focussed more inside the analysis. But even more important was the maternal transference which had first shown itself in the Grave dream. This was now becoming more firmly established, in relation to the baby who thinks he's been weaned because he bit the nipple. This fierce, domineering baby-within-Hamlet took us back also to the Ghost dream and the source of male aggression against his mother which was expressed in it. Then in the last session he had accused me (perhaps with some justification, I wondered) of not being strong enough to contain his aggression during the Mousetrap. The extent to which this was directed against me as his analytic mother was now becoming much clearer. He truly felt that I carried the scar of his aggression.

Then one evening, Hamlet came in flushed and excited, announcing in the same breath that he had beaten Nando in a game of squash and had had a dream.

In this dream, *he was in a submarine with his friends from the play – Rosenfeld, Gildstein, Seaman and Peacock. They were taking the submarine on a trip to Hertford to be reconditioned. It seemed quite natural that the way to Hertford was underwater. But then they started fighting over who was in control of the vessel, and Hamlet was afraid it was going to crash. He realized it was vitally important to save the black box and take it to Hertford so they could see what was going wrong with the submarine. But he could not get the importance of this over to his friends, who continued arsing about, so he seized the black box and escaped from the upper hatch.*

It was not quite clear in the dream whether the danger was caused by the friends fighting for control or whether there was something inherently wrong with the vessel. Hamlet saw easily enough that the dream described his own need to be "reconditioned" after the fiasco of the Mousetrap, with the friends representing his own masturbatory fingers generating delusions of omnipotence. *With divine ambition puff'd.* And the crash described his own sudden deflation (with possibly some reference to drugs and Forte's party, and "tripping"). But he seemed to recognize the need to get help from Hertford and to provide the information about his inmost functioning which was contained in the black box.

Clearly, there was a pun in the name Hertford on the lines of something like "heartfelt", which could be linked to our discussions about sincerity. Hamlet's dream diagnosed his illness in terms of the need to get out of an enclosed state, back to a condition of real emotionality at the heart of his mystery (the black box) – not a status-conscious identity such as that stimulated by the Mrs Forte model of achievement with its "tripping", "crashing", and "arsing about" irresponsibly. In the dream he had had to make a choice between opposing sets of values. Also, as in the original Grave dream, these values indicated that he could not do it all by himself, in his usual directorial manner. *To thine own self be true, thou canst not then be false to any man.* Yes, I thought, this Submarine dream confirmed that the analysis was under way again.

Hamlet then said he had another association to the dream. There was a nurse on Ophelia's ward named Sister Hertford whom Nando had mentioned. In fact, said Hamlet, Ophelia was said to be much better and was due to come out of hospital next week. He said this almost reluctantly, with some apprehension, and when I pointed this out to him, confessed he was terrified of accidentally encountering her. There was no question of a deliberate meeting of course. He had felt a gloomy satisfaction at the thought that she was restrained in the ward under supervision, while he was at the same time paying his regular penitential visits to me in my secluded basement. He would have preferred this arrangement to go on indefinitely, for ever.

Now she would be loose in the world again, and even though he knew they would try to avoid each other, his security was gone and his passive morbid resignation might no longer rest unchallenged. He couldn't quite see why, since he had neither hope nor desire of ever resuming their relationship. Yet his dream had suggested he had in mind some presiding nursing or healing figure who was common to both of them, could read the black box of both himself and Ophelia, perhaps on the lines of this Sister Hertford or of the old woman in the Grave dream who had said "tears shall be your recreation".

The session after this, Hamlet told me that his mother had been to visit Ophelia. In fact she had been several times, but he had never spoken directly to her about it. But Nando told him casually that Gertrude had left a bowl of daffodil bulbs for Ophelia to take with her when she came out, and Hamlet had had a dream about it.

In the dream, *he was walking behind a woman wearing long white robes and headdress, perhaps like a nun, along what seemed like an interminable labyrinth of dark corridors. In pure white robes like very sanctity. Eventually they came to a door, and as the woman stopped to open it, Hamlet saw she was carrying a bowl of daffodil bulbs newly in flower. The woman entered and shut the door, apparently oblivious of Hamlet's presence. It seemed that he was unable to open the door for himself, and was about to turn away in despair, when he realized there was a clear window in the door so he could at least see inside. When he looked through he had to blink because the light was dazzling by contrast with the dark corridor. It was a large room with many beds, and he realized this must be the hospital ward where Ophelia was; but the room seemed decorated as if for a party, with bouquets of flowers and ribbons festooned all over it. There was a loud buzz of gay chatter, but when the white-robed woman entered there was a hush. She put the bowl down on a lace-covered table. Ophelia was standing behind it.*

Then the woman said, "What was lost has now been found", and Ophelia said, gravely, "Welcome, as spring to the earth." And all the girls in the room, in their nightdresses, brought garlands of flowers and hung them on Ophelia. Ophelia jumped up on the bed behind her, holding out her arms, and began to sing:

> *O Proserpina! tell me now*
> > *It is gone, it is gone*
> *How should I a true love know*
> > *From another one?*
>
> *My spirits followed you down below;*
> > *I was numb, I was numb.*
> *My own soul was the embryo*
> > *And so, undone.*
>
> *Imprisoned by the winter's flaw*
> > *In the grave, in the grave*
> *Till you unlatched the chamber door*
> > *And my sins forgave.*
>
> *I never knew how still it was*
> > *In the ground, in the ground*
> *I was nerveless, listless, voiceless,*
> > *Without a sound.*
>
> *Bound I was by that deadly spell*
> > *Like a stone, like a stone;*
> *You promised me that out of hell*
> > *At last I'd come.*
>
> *Released by hope I saw that I could*
> > *Let it be, let it be;*
> *Because I would at last reward*
> > *Your faith in me.*

When Ophelia had finished her song she beckoned two other girls up on to the bed and placed garlands on them, then tossed flowers to others, and they all started to leap from bed to bed exuberantly, giggling and laughing. Meanwhile Hamlet remained with his face *rivetted to the window, feeling as though he were "in a courtroom waiting for sentence to be pronounced." He wanted to sneak away but his legs would not move. Then to his horror the woman with the daffodils started to walk towards him, and he turned and ran back away down the corridor.*

This, then, was the beginning rather than the end of Hamlet's "recreation". After he had recounted the dream, he was quiet and thoughtful. I asked him why he had been "horrified" when the woman walked towards him — was he expecting punishment, or reprimand from her? He said no, he was terrified that she was coming to let him in. As if she, too, had expectations of him. I suggested these expectations might constitute shame or remorse on his part, and a re-awakening such as he imagined Ophelia to have undergone in his dream. This mental activity was, if sincere, more disturbing than the self-inflicted carceration of blame or punishment. *Her unshaped speech moved the hearers to collection.*

Then Hamlet said, stirring awkwardly on the couch, "It's weird but I feel as if a great weight was pressing down on me. I can't get rid of the feeling left by that dream, it hangs on. In fact I feel incredibly sleepy. If I stay here I don't think I can stop myself going to sleep."

He roused himself, however, as it was in fact nearly the end of the session. But before getting up, looking out of the window, he remarked in a tone of wonder "how blue the sky was today". I pointed out, with a heightened interest, that the sky visible from the consulting room window was in fact grey and heavy. His vision was a subjective or dream reponse, associated with his looking through the window of the ward at the brightness of the revived condition attained by Ophelia. But whereas in the actual dream he had felt excluded and disgraced, the bright window in the consulting room seemed to offer a prospect on his own regeneration. His subjective vision, I felt sure, indicated his hope that the baby in him could, through the analysis, be rescued from the grave-rectum. The light might shine on him too, and wake him out of his deep sleep. On this note of resurgent optimism (which later, alas, I came to view somewhat differently) we parted, I believed, on the verge of a breakthrough.

CHAPTER SEVEN

The Tempest

> **Hamlet**: Sir, in my heart there was a kind of fighting
> That would not let me sleep. Methought I lay
> Worse than the mutines in the bilboes ...
> Being thus benetted round with villainies –
> Or ere I could make a prologue to my brains,
> They had begun the play. (V. ii. 4-6, 29-31)

Horacio offers insufficient support over Hamlet's self-denigration in the Tempest dream and is then shocked and hurt by Hamlet's hypocritical way of breaking off the analysis.

Ophelia came home shortly before the Easter break. I did not see Hamlet for three weeks. On the first session of the new term he came in muffled to the hilt in a long black scarf wound round his neck and ears, dark glasses, and a zipped up leather jacket. He moved with uncharacteristic slowness and lay down silently and lugubriously. Then from the depths of the scarf came a low, strangled humming. For a moment I wondered whether he was sobbing, but he then explained that he "had a stinking cold and was drowning in catarrh; his brain was buzzing".

A strange humming about my ears. There was still a question in my mind about the humming, which sounded somehow familiar. I asked him what it was. He didn't seem to realize at first that he had been humming anything specifically, and moved his jaws to discover what it was, then said in a tone of mild boredom: "It's just some old Beatles song." I asked which one, and he replied reluctantly, "It's one called 'Help'." When I asked for the words, he said he couldn't remember, so I reminded him they went something like:

> How can you laugh when you know I'm down ...
> Help! You know I need somebody,
> Help! You know I need someone.

He seemed mildly amused and said, rather contemptuously, "I didn't think you were supposed to divulge your cultural interests." I suggested to him that he was "drowning in catarrh", namely some flood of emotionality, and had made the significant step of asking me for help, although I had had to fish for the confession.

"Oh yes – Dr Horacio, fisher of men!", he teased, and broke into a violent fit of coughing, during which he took off his glasses and blew his nose. When I asked why he was wearing the glasses he said he had a stye in his eye, and then, after further prompting, confessed he "couldn't stand people looking straight at him" – he felt intolerably exposed. *A strange fish.* In fact he had distanced himself from his group of friends and spent the vacation shut up at home.

"Even old Claude was making an effort – though it was transparent he was acting on instructions from my mother. She'd obviously told him I was depressed, so he'd been racking his brains to see what he could do to draw me out of myself, and he came up with the idea of taking me sailing on the Welsh Harp – as if I was a ten-year-old or something. He's just not switched on. But my mother was dead keen for me to go, she practically begged me, so I thought what the hell, it's no big deal anyway, so I went – it was easier than not going. The next day of course we both went down with flu." He coughed again and laughed ironically, "Yes, at last we found something in common!"

Nevertheless I pointed this out as perhaps a new turn in their relationship, and suggested Hamlet in some part of himself had appreciated his sympathetic intentions.

"His intentions – O God, his *intentions*! There's always something behind Claude's gestures, he can't do anything spontaneously. So what, who cares ... if it suits him to play daddy, that's OK by me – even if he hasn't the foggiest idea how to go about it. At least it keeps my mother quiet."

I also noted that Hamlet's mention of the sailing episode, together with his own appearance, defensively wrapped in leather and glasses, was reminiscent yet again of the Ghost-pilot. In the original dream he had found this uniform rather threatening, and the other time he had imitated it in order to appear threatening himself; but this time it seemed more of a refuge. He agreed that what he needed was a refuge; he couldn't face any of the "old crowd":

"Even people I don't know, I feel must be staring at me. I went into Hall on Wednesday for dinner – I hadn't been for ages – and I could see people – well, *looking* at me, laughing – not out loud of course, but I knew what they were thinking."

What did he believe they were thinking?

"Well I knew they must have been to see that fucking play. They know all about me, and Ophelia, and everything. They know exactly what was going on, and they're thinking what a pansyfaced prick I was to play the whole thing in public, expecting to get idolized like some tit of a pop star. Why couldn't I keep my sordid little secrets to myself like everybody else, then I wouldn't look such a fool." *The rugged Pyrrhus*.

He spoke vehemently and contemptuously of himself, ending with another episode of coughing and sneezing. Then, in a flatter, more detached tone of voice, he explained that after the sailing afternoon he had taken to his bed in his new room in his parents' flat, and been content to lie there day after day in a fluey or exhausted state, staring out of the newly installed skylight and listening to music through headphones plugged firmly over his ears.

"Fabulous things, clouds", he began, in a theatrical manner, slightly sarcastic: "the way their shape is always changing. The frieze of life. You can see them as different characters, or else as the same character going through a whole succession of experiences. *The camel, the weasel and the whale.* You know - life events. The really fascinating thing is the total meaninglessness of it all – the clouds never let you forget that."

The meaninglessness, I stressed, was an important recognition. He sounded offended at my taking him at his word, saying: "Actually I got down some pretty good poems about it – don't worry, I'm not going to read them to you, I know they're not your style. My mother, of course, would be dying to have a look. She put her head round the door – pretending to see if I wanted dinner or something – saw I was writing – 'Oh Hamlet!' she twitters, 'you're writing again! I'm so glad.' What the hell is she glad for? Good job she can't see what I *do* write. I make quite sure of that." *The book and volume of my brain.*

This was said with a hard determination, making sure I took note. I asked him what he thought would disturb his mother in his poems, and he said she'd "probably think I was going to commit suicide or something – she's so literal minded. I have to protect her from myself. Anyway I hope by now she's learned I've got to have my privacy."

I told Hamlet I accepted his despair had to be taken seriously; his sincerity in this was not in doubt. During the holiday when I had not been available he had at least managed to accept the refuge of his parents' home, where he felt he could hide away his intolerable sense of meaninglessness and not be assaulted by humiliation (as with his fellow-students).

"Well actually", he said, "it was a relief to get back into digs – I would definitely have died of claustrophobia if I'd lived at home another ten minutes. It was the dreadful way she kept fluttering her eyelashes at me, anxiously, all the time trying not to interfere, not to *say* anything. And Claude wasn't much better, he's gone kind of soft. 'Untimely death of student – suffocated by pity'." *Here, Hamlet, take my napkin, rub thy brows.*

I hoped, however, that once the analysis was re-established after the usual distancing of the break, we would get more information about the nature of his depression. But it took a surprisingly long time to regain his confidence. Guilt and shame were not enough to explain the restless and persecutory quality of his depression; they did not account for its deep humiliation. Like a suppurating sore, it was aggravated by every slight contact from his intimate friends – in particular every expression of concern. *Their great guilt bites their spirits.* As in the Mousetrap dream, he felt surrounded by faces "leering and laughing" at him. Consequently he avoided contact with his former circle, shutting himself away in his room or in a remote corner of the library, pretending to work. As if in response to this, he received a note from Professor Polack inviting him to contribute to a journal whose editorial board he was on.

"Even he feels sorry for me", said Hamlet bitterly. "As always, he's got it all wrong. He thinks I'm burying myself in intellectual pursuits to work off my Great Guilt. The reality is much more crude and basic. I just want to be left alone. I don't want anything to do with any of them. I can't stand their fucking pity. Let them indulge themselves, feeling all warm and compassionate about everybody – it's fine, if that's what turns them on – but leave me out of it. I'm not going to play that game."

He continued in this gloomy and irritable vein for several weeks. His cold, with complications of cough and sinusitis, took a long time to subside, and instead, a virulent rash of spots erupted over his face, beyond anything he had ever suffered before. He remained wrapped in the black scarf as spring progressed. Meanwhile he claimed to be doing no academic work apart from the minimum hack-work with which he could get by without drawing attention to himself. I gathered that he was also writing a great deal of poetry, which of course he showed no-one, and which he kept in a locked black box – "yeah, like the Submarine dream", he pre-empted my saying.

And the day after this, he did finally bring a dream which clarified what I felt to be the suppurating sore within him:

"*I was in this boat with Ros and Gil. Actually it was an Enterprise dinghy like the one I went out in with Claude in the Easter holiday. The idea was that we were going fishing; we had a trawling net over the side. But Ros and Gil were arsing about, moving piles of books from one side of the dinghy to the other, saying they had to get the ballast right, and taking swigs from a bottle of whisky which they* kept passing between them. And Ophelia was there too, sitting in the prow of the boat with her sheet of yellow hair spreading out in the breeze. She seemed to be waving and egging them on."

And what was Hamlet himself doing?

"I was at the tiller, so I couldn't move. Then Gil noticed there was a catch in the net, so I turned the boat into the wind and we all started to haul with all our strength. In fact the boat nearly capsized as we got it on board. Ros said, "Bugger this rotten leaking carcass of a butt.""

Here Hamlet paused uncomfortably, then continued:

"And it turned out to be a man, a black man – I know what you're going to say. But the thing was – not only was he dripping wet, he was covered in seaweed and barnacles. He looked like some weird sea-creature from the depths. Ros and Gil started to pull the net off him, pissing about and making jokes about how he looked half fish, half monster. But now the wind had really got up, and although I had the tiller again it didn't seem to control the boat any more – the sheets were all entangled with the ropes of the net, and the sails were flapping like mad."

And Ophelia?

"*Ophelia seemed to have vanished. I never noticed her after the beginning. There was just the mainsail flapping furiously over us, making a terrible din:*

> *The pinioned sail roared loudly overhead,*
> *And foolishly the fishes beat the floor*
> *For kissing of their fins, yet still the ship*
> *Bent on towards its goal. Like unback'd colts*
> *They prick'd their ears, advanced their eyes,*
> *And lifted up their noses, smelling music.*
> *Plunging and tacking through water and air, the boat*
> *Drew them half wading, half flying to the water's edge*
> *Where finally it lodged amongst the reeds."*

This dream, I thought, was a fascinating history or review of Hamlet's sexual awakening: from masturbatory experimentation (his fingers represented by Ros and Gil), through discovery of the "monstrous" genitals (the black box) and the sense of being out of control with the flapping mainsail taking over the boat/

body - Ophelia having turned into the sail and taken on a somewhat frightening aspect. Also of course the whole "enterprise" (as in the name of the dinghy class) came under the auspices of the father who had introduced him to it, which made a link with his earlier dreams of the Ghost-pilot and the "hovering" father in the Mousetrap dream who had tried to discipline his son's mania.

"It was you I called a fisher of men", said Hamlet, coughing. "This is what your fishing trips lead to."

It was more, I said, Hamlet fishing in his own unconscious, to discover lost or unknown parts of himself. As so often before, I reminded him that it was *his* dream – no invention of mine. In this dream he did seem to be revising and repairing his attack on *A Midsummer Night's Dream*; it showed how he had worked his way out of his claustrophobia, carrying further his escape in the Submarine dream, and becoming this strange barnacled black man. *A fish-like monster.* It was clear that this man, like a merman in a fairy tale, was an alter-ego of his own.

"Not simple racism?" he said bluntly.

Possibly racist, I said, but not "simply". Any more than the sail was "simply" feminist. Both seemed to represent essential aspects or qualities within himself, vital to the functioning of his boat: one making a link with undersea richness, the other catching the winds of spiritual movement. *The fringed curtains of thine eye advance.* As an image of womanhood, I was interested in the persecutory quality of the sail. The expanse of light-catching material (like Ophelia's yellow hair) was reminiscent also of Sister Hertford's flowing white robes in his dream.

"And of my mother in the Mousetrap dream", he added. "And of Claude too if you like in his fancy silk dressing gown." *A king of shreds and patches.*

In that dream, of course, Gertrude had seemed to collapse under his onslaught and Claude had given him a stern warning. Whereas here, it was the Ophelia-sail itself which took on the role of somehow rebuking or frightening him. Yet the sail had not actually capsized the boat, nor had the confusion in the boat resulted in Hamlet's having to escape from a hatch as in the Submarine dream. In fact, Hamlet pointed out, the boat seemed to have a mind of its own, independent of its human sailors, and they felt themselves irresistibly drawn to the water's edge which was the boat's goal. Yes, I agreed, it was a dream of discovery rather than of omnipotence: of following desires rather than manipulating excitement. The dream also gave us a clue as to his feeling of rejection by Ophelia for being an ugly barnacle-man: when his identity was finally fished up and exposed to view, he was (he felt) clearly no match for her shimmering sail-beauty.

This was certainly a new and hopeful departure. After Hamlet had left, I had a few minutes' break, and walked up to the High Street with the excuse of buying a packet of cigarettes, but really to enjoy the bright spring sunshine. On the way there I indulged myself in feeling pleased, even elated. The tide was turning. On the way back, however, I noticed a certain frustration in myself. I was eager to facilitate Hamlet's recovery, but despite his plea for help as in the song, and his dubbing me a fisher of men, I suspected I was a little unnecessary. There was something tenuous about our relationship. We were not working *together*; his dreams were doing all the work, and I did nothing but confirm their significance. If only I could do more to pull him forwards, now we were on the right track! I felt almost impatient in my optimism.

Then to the next session, Hamlet brought a dream which seemed to follow on directly from this Tempest dream, filling out its implications regarding his own identity:

"*I was lying on the shore, alone. I could feel the mud in my toes and fingers, stretched out. I felt I was pinioned there. I was looking up at the sun filtering through the canopy of leaves overhead, and there was a strange music enveloping me on all sides. I couldn't tell where it was coming from; it seemed to come out of the ground and the air at the same time.*"

Here again was the idea of music holding the elements of the dream together, providing its meaningfulness. *This music crept by me on the waters*. I asked if the experience seemed pleasurable, or painful?

"Neither", he said emphatically. "It was paralysing. My senses were all bound up. I couldn't move away, or stop listening. I realized it was a dream. The weird thing was, when I woke up, I remembered the music very vividly, not as a tune but as a physical sensation, and I had this intense longing to get back into the dream. At the same time I knew I was still asleep, but not in *that* dream. *I was still stuck in the mud, and my body was covered in barnacles and seaweed, as though I was growing or rather rotting into the beach like some old piece of driftwood. It was then I realized that I stank. And a voice began to sing my song for me, to the words in my head:*

> *Full fathom five my father lies,*
>   *Developing pearl and weed;*
> *Whilst Ros and Gil are under hatches*
>   *Safely stoned in bed.*
>
> *The reasonable shore is mud*
>   *And I alone am conscious*
> *Now the ooze has belched me up*
>   *How infinite my loss.*
>
> *In dismay I mourned the change*
>   *I cried to dream again*
> *Without the music sweet and strange*
>   *I'm but a sot like him.*
>
> *He used to stroke me, taught me how*
>   *To know my words, at first;*
> *My lasting profit is that now*
>   *I know how to curse.*
>
> *So fill my skin with pinches black,*
>   *Make me strange stuff -*
> *A canker'd, fuming maniac*
>   *A true moon-calf.*
>
> *The devils hiss me into madness,*
>   *The music must be free;*
> *O Prospero! this thing of darkness*
>   *I acknowledge me.*

This curious lament, founded on his identification with the sea-monster-man of the previous dream, filled me with hope about the possibility of Hamlet's really coming to terms with his own "darkness" (omnipotence). His realization that he "stank" was an extension of his barnacle-man identification, and he clearly felt himself rejected by both Ophelia and the Prospero figure whom he associated with the use and abuse of language. *Words, words, words.* In this Prospero we could see aspects of Polack and of myself in the analysis, both representing Ophelia's guardian – the father behind her – who seemed to Hamlet to have pronounced him inadequate. *A fishmonger.* There was also, of course, a link with his own father who had introduced him to the "enterprise", as in the name of the dinghy. Now, taking the two dreams together, this masculine element seemed to be more an integral part of Ophelia herself. This went along with his growing appreciation of the power of femininity. This was the music which needed to be free (as in the Museum dream) - a reversal of his old directorial mode. *Sweet bells jangled out of tune.* My enthusiasm increased as I felt we were getting nearer the source of his intense sense of humiliation: was it, then, Ophelia whom he believed to be always laughing at him?

"Of course Ophelia is a brilliant musician in her own right I told you that", Hamlet mumbled, clearly finding this latter interpretation extremely uncomfortable; "but showing off isn't the same as laughing at *me*." However he noted other links with the Winter's Tale dream, such as Ophelia's hymn to Proserpina as the agent of release from inner darkness, linked with the figure of Sister Hertford (heartfelt). I agreed he seemed here to be making a similar appeal here to myself in the form of Prospero.

I also showed how the "darkness" or "madness" acknowledged in the dream had expressed itself somatically in the spots on his face, his cold, and his wrapping himself up in the scarf not so unlike a man caught in a net or a piece of driftwood wrapped in seaweed. *Creep under the gabardine.* He squirmed at this, but over the next week or two his health made a noticeable improvement, and he was more cheerful than I had known him. Bedded down in the mud, perhaps he was metabolizing a sea-change. For the Tempest dream was, I believed, a dream about the making of poetry as well as love, and I wondered whether Hamlet had perhaps been working seriously at his own writing. Certainly I was very hopeful about these signs of a new dependence on creative internal objects who could bring the music into his life to transform his own curses. This would indicate the possibility of a genuine mental prosperity on the horizon.

However, this was not to be. Our progress was abruptly cut short. Perhaps not so abruptly, for during the final weeks of his analysis I could sense him tiptoeing away, out of contact with me, distancing himself. *The interim is mine.* His manner was pleasant and polite, but he was cocooned in a type of indolence or passivity. The intimacy of the transference, which had been growing so strongly, seemed to evaporate. Indeed, looking back on it, even by the Tempest dream the transference had lost the maternal quality which had been its most hopeful recent development. Instead of the baby-Hamlet's attachment to his analytic mother, we were back to the little boy wrestling with his analytic father – and now accepting (unwillingly) the impotence of his immaturity. In itself this was, of course, a useful beginning. But this kind of dependence seemed to stimulate an underlying irritation with me, amounting almost to persecution, though not of the old explosive paranoid type, and carefully veiled by politeness. *Following the king's pleasure.* The precise cause puzzled me greatly – was it really that he couldn't stand the painfulness of these new feelings of ugliness and humiliation? He must know – we all did – that that kind of suffering was good for him, it was the only way forward. And (as he once told me himself) he was not a coward. It was more, I mused, as though he felt triumphed over by my eagerness – as though I were jubilant over his fall, rather than nurturing his development. Again I regretted the fading of the maternal transference, though I assumed it would be only temporary. I expected him to oscillate on this threshold for some time, as with our struggle over the Grave. Instead, he slipped away from me altogether.

The warning signs first appeared when Hamlet recounted to me his first (inevitable) chance encounter with Ophelia after she had come out of hospital. It was, of course, what he had been dreading; but I was convinced that once it had happened he would soon assimilate the experience into his life and it would prove fruitful in the long run, however uncomfortable at the time. He began wryly enough and with a tinge of humour:

"I saw her under the arches in the market. She was standing by a pillar looking at the rain pelting down in the square. My head crept right down into my scarf, in fact it's given me a crick in the neck. *The snail's shelly pain.* There were loads of people about. She had her back to me and I thought I might get away without being noticed."

Here he paused and seemed reluctant to continue.

"But I didn't", he said with a note of finality. "She turned round and saw me."

He said this as though his doom were sealed. I was puzzled at his making such a drama of it.

"Of course she was a bit embarrassed. Only for a few seconds. Then she had a good look at me. I knew she was feeling sorry for me, because I am such a wreck. *Th'observed of all observers, quite, quite down.* And then I realized, with absolute certainty, that it had to be all over between us. I suppose till then, I must have secretly imagined we might somehow have picked it up again. But I just couldn't stand her pitying me, after the way things used to be."

Is that all? I wondered to myself. We were, of course, back in the familiar territory of his assuming with "absolute certainty" that he "knew" Ophelia's feelings, on evidence which ranged from the slender to the non-existent. This time, however, I suspected it was not his old tyrannical grandiosity, but an excuse for something else. We could at least, I said, investigate the sincerity of his own reaction.

"No, no," he insisted earnestly; "this time I really *do* know. There's no need for you to smooth over my failures. I've been thinking about it a lot since it happened, and I feel I can step out now, and get on with life. I can face things better now I know where we stand."

Something about this made me ask, when *did* the meeting with Ophelia take place? He replied furtively that it was about ten days ago, and when I asked why he hadn't told me before, mumbled some feeble excuses about how it hadn't actually come to his mind in the sessions and "hadn't seemed that important at the time, it was only thinking over it ..." etc. This particular type of dishonesty had never occurred with Hamlet before, and it made me uneasy. Previous barriers to communication between us had always been of a tangible sort, demonstrably resulting from his omnipotence. This type of non-communication was more like a vacuum. *If Hamlet from himself be taken away, he is not Hamlet but his madness.* I would have to evolve some new method of bridging the new madness.

However I was not to be given the chance. A few days after that session, I received a letter from Hamlet informing me that he had decided to terminate his analysis:

Dear Dr Horacio,

I am writing to thank you for all you have done to give me some real confidence in myself. You will understand what I mean when I say that now I feel ready at last to face the rat-race of life. Without you I couldn't have done it. You were the only person I could rely on not to play on my sensitivities like a pipe, or to pretend you were suffering with me when really you didn't care. Above all, I have found the experience of being in analysis to be a wonderful training in self-observation. That, I know, will be an invaluable qualification for the future.

Meanwhile, since we are no longer bound by the psycho-analytic code, I expect you might like to see a few lines from a long autobiographical poem I am writing, as a kind of farewell present:

> I don't want to be
> like you, Forte:
> a lapwing running away
> with the shell on its head.
> The expectancy of an MG
> and other childish toys
> won't satisfy me.

> My own ambition is divine, and puffing out,
> makes mouths at the invisible event.
> The yet unknowing world shall see
> my shell will be
> around, above, within me.
> The readiness is all.
>
> Adieu! with love from Hamlet.

And farewell it was, for the next eight years. Such was my dismissal by the prince: courteously, the barriers were drawn between his inner self and me. Frequently at first, then intermittently throughout that period, the memory of Hamlet would recur as a variable dose of miserable bewilderment. I could make no sense of his departure. Why had he done it? Here again was the lonely, only child; but instead of reaching out as when I had first met him, he had chosen to shut himself away, knowingly, in his MG-type shell of supposed worldly invulnerability, where he would not be prey to disturbing emotional relationships. After all our work to release him from a seriously claustrophobic state, his grandiosity had merely taken another form. And then the unconscious hypocrisy of it – to pretend to thank *me* for this new pseudo-independence! He might as well thank me for kicking me in the balls, or stabbing me in the heart. While I was left unweaponed, with no right to reply.

CHAPTER EIGHT

The King and Queen

> **King**: In the corrupted currents of this world
> Offence's gilded hand may shove by justice,
> And oft 'tis seen the wicked prize itself
> Buys out the law. But 'tis not so above:
> There is no shuffling, there the action lies
> In his true nature, and we ourselves compell'd
> Even to the teeth and forehead of our faults
> To give in evidence. (III. iii. 57-64)

Breaching his own analytic technique, Horacio dines with Hamlet's parents and discovers something rotten in the state of Denmark which mirrors personal problems of his own, that he now suspects might have interfered with his relationship with Hamlet.

Despite Hamlet's farewell letter, I kept his regular sessions available for two weeks in case he should suddenly choose to come back. It would be hard for me to say whether I was more hurt or mystified by his sudden departure. It was as though I had been in the process of pulling someone who had fallen overboard back on the ship, when they let go my hand and slowly sank from view. *Not waving but drowning*. Hamlet waved goodbye, apparently unaware that he was drowning. And I, too, sometimes felt I was drowning in a welter of painful confusion. Had I somehow conspired with him in the delusion that he was cured, or at any rate set on his way as a creative writer – ready in fact to write his autobiography? Had I given the impression that his distress at Ophelia's illness, in both somatic and dream-terms, had earned him some sort of absolution from his sins, which could then be packaged away into the past? *A special providence.*

No, I could find nothing in my soul-searching of those weeks to explain Hamlet's sliding away into his shell, or to match the intensity of my degree of hurt at his complacent and hypocritical letter. I was impatient for information, for new light on the matter. So when I contacted his parents to inform them that he had broken off his analysis (of which, as I suspected, they were not aware), and Gertrude invited me to discuss it with them over dinner at their home, I accepted with very little hesitation. I told myself that what I would normally have considered a breach of technique (given that I had by no means given up hope of his return) was excusable in these peculiar circumstances. Moreover, I found the temptation to see the Danes' new flat irresistible, especially as my own home seemed a particularly cheerless and disturbing place at that moment in time.

It was a fine evening in early summer when I sauntered slowly over the top of the Heath, still alive with strollers and dogwalkers, past the usual gaggle of Saturday night teenagers congregating round Whitestone Pond. As I walked I meditated on the empty house I'd left behind me in Flask Walk. My daughters were away at pony camp for the weekend, and for the first time my wife had openly gone off with her lover. How was it, I wondered, that I had not seen – had refused to see – the extent of our alienation from one another, before now? Beatrice had seemed almost surprised at my concern. Was it some sort of narcissism on my part, that assumed our relationship was invulnerable – was I really perhaps what Hamlet was always calling me, an "old romantic"? Occupied by disturbing and unresolvable musings, I arrived at the Danes' new flat in Redington Road.

Their flat, which Hamlet had complained about as being poky and cramped, was spacious, elegant and luxuriously appointed. It had been converted with exquisite taste, retaining early nineteenth-century features such as a huge marble fireplace and carefully restored plaster mouldings. These were combined with modern open-planning and light. The airy, split-level hexagonal hallway, floored in white marble, had a short flight of wide, open stairs up one side (and a doorway off them, leading presumably to Hamlet's "cupboard"). All the room doors led off the central skylit hall, including a noble archway to the large parquet-floored Persian-carpeted sitting-cum-dining room, with a view onto the garden through a glass wall at the end. I admired on behalf of my wife the gleaming steel of the kitchen range and appurtenances, visible through another doorway. The heavy scent of honeysuckle wafted through the open French windows in the gloaming.

An amiable-looking, elderly serving woman whom Gertrude addressed affectionately as "Lise *chérie*", came round with a tray of exotic homemade hors d'oeuvres, while Claude descended to the basement and returned with several dark, dusty bottles of red wine. He set these on the dining table and opened two of them.

"I'm sorry your wife couldn't come, Dr Horacio", said Gertrude, who was wearing a silk blouse and trousers, and jewelled slippers. She seemed fluttery and anxious. Claude, in a black polo-neck sweater, looked distinguished and genial, with his curly grey hair. For a moment, impressed by their welcome, I almost wondered whether it would be appropriate to mention my own personal troubles. But Claude, with either exquisite manners or extreme tact, rendered any such confession unnecessary:

"It wouldn't have been fair to inflict this post-mortem on her", he said, handing me the Tio Pepe I had asked for, then pouring himself a glass of wine.

No, I thought, I was there in a capacity of courtesy rather than of personal intimacy. Without any further preliminaries, Gertrude asked me directly why Hamlet had stopped his analysis. "It's not because he is – perhaps – able to manage now without it, is it?" she asked, carefully avoiding the word "cured".

I replied that I did not understand it myself. It had happened when he had just begun to work seriously at it, and when I had been feeling most optimistic about our chances of progress. No, I did not think he was all right in any other than a superficial sense; in fact, the way he had broken it off made me feel quite worried about him.

"Worried in what sense – you don't think he might do himself some harm, do you?" asked his mother quickly. "It was such a terrible shock when Ophelia slit her wrists – none of us had foreseen anything like that. Poor Antony became an old man overnight." *Hugger mugger.*

I reassured her that now, my anxieties about Hamlet were to do with character development, rather than with mental illness.

"It seemed to me", said Claude, "that he had become very much better. You must have done something for him, Dr Horacio. I had quite a pleasant outing with him during the Easter vacation when we went sailing. Almost nostalgic, like old times. As though I were a human being again, even in his eyes." *He returned, checking at his voyage.*

"But it was evident that he was still very unhappy", said Gertrude. "It wasn't really like old times. He had lost his spirit. He just shut himself in his room, moping."

"Well it's a good thing he did lose his spirit, in my view", said Claude. "There were times when I could have murdered him. And I suspect he was pretty nasty to Ophelia over the pregnancy business. I think he was depressed because he was feeling guilty – and that can only be a good thing." *So full of jealousy is guilt.*

"What surprised me was how little he said about Ophelia", said Gertrude. "He knew I'd been to see her when she was in hospital, several times. But he never asked me how she was, never even asked about the miscarriage."

"It isn't likely he'd have talked to you about it, in the circumstances, is it – he'd find out from Nando", said Claude.

"But", continued Gertrude in a puzzled tone, "it was the same with her. She never mentioned Hamlet either. I asked Sister Hertford and she said the same. It was as though he'd gone out of her life."

I could hardly refrain from expressing my surprise when I heard Gertrude speak of Ophelia's "miscarriage". Clearly Hamlet had not been aware of this – had not had the curiosity to find out. Meanwhile Claude was addressing his wife in a significant and pointed manner:

"I think myself", he said, "that we were too keen to push them together in the first place. You were, in particular, my dear – you and Antony. It looked like the ideal finale to our family intimacy."

From this point in the conversation I began to find my position in our little triangle extremely uncomfortable. The Danes began by treating me rather like the trusted family lawyer who is privy to the various skeletons in the family cupboard. But as Hamlet's analyst (or failed analyst) the situation was far more complicated and uneasy.

Gertrude leaned slightly in my direction with a confidential air and looked at her husband with a sort of provocative, amused defiance, saying:

"Claude's still jealous, you see, Dr Horacio. He's jealous because he believes I had a little affair with Antony once – at a time, I may say, when he was so busy building up his business to be the biggest in Britain that he wasn't really aware of my existence."

"That's a great exaggeration", said Claude, ruffled. "And Antony wasn't the only one I had reason to worry about. But you're not taking my point, Gertrude – which is, that Hamlet and Ophelia are only a couple of inexperienced teenagers. Nobody gets married that young these days."

"Nobody said they had to get married!" exclaimed his wife. "There would have been plenty of time for that later. And we didn't get married so young ourselves, did we?" she reminded him, somewhat accusingly.

"That was because of the war", he said authoritatively. "I needed to get established first."

He looked at me as if to seek my confirmation, and I was unsure how to respond, finding myself to be an involuntary witness of a private quarrel, yet aware that each of them regarded me as an essential ingredient. Possibly, I felt, my presence even acted as a catalyst.

"Claude's always paid too much attention to being established", said Gertrude to me. "We could have been half as rich and had twice as many children and been twice as happy." She spoke surprisingly sharply, and clearly pained him.

"Are you really saying you haven't been happy with me?" he asked, looking genuinely hurt, his mouth drooping mournfully. At this Gertrude softened immediately and said "No, no - you know that's not what I mean at all. We've been very happy, more than many people. We've been lucky."

"We've been lucky, I might say, because of working hard", he corrected her. "I wanted to give my son what my father gave me, and more."

"Of course, and you have", she said soothingly. "Nobody could say Hamlet hasn't had every possible opportunity, every advantage. And love. I just mean, perhaps you even worked *too* hard. All those years of you making big money and us entertaining the whole world in our London mansion – what was it all for?"

"It wasn't the money – you know that", said Claude, irritated that his wife should bring up this commonplace misconception. He began to walk up and down in front of the fireplace, gesticulating with his free hand (the other still holding his glass) in a way that reminded me of Hamlet. "It was the quality of the business that interested me. I told my researchers I wanted drugs that were economically viable as well as effective – drugs that could really be made available. And I always employed the best – and having got them, I wanted to keep them; so I made sure they wanted to stay. My company, Dr Horacio, was regarded as a model of its kind. Gertrude seems to have forgotten all the effort I put in, from the very beginning, toward improving the working conditions. I don't mean only the industrial aspects; I was one of the first to implement the incentives for better morale, which were just experimental at the time – rewards for length of service, workers' councils, transferrable pensions, profit-sharing, and so on. I wanted them to understand it was *their* company as much as mine. I knew that efficiency depended on work satisfaction and loyalty to the company. The result was that when I sold to Universal my company was an asset in every way. They were lucky to get it!"

He paused for a moment, impressively, holding up his glass, and nodded toward me before adding: "And I never would have sold if Hamlet had taken any interest in it." *The king drinks to Hamlet's better breath.*

Like a mother with a stormy child, Gertrude went up and stroked his arm in a placatory gesture, whilst smiling at me apologetically yet confidentially in a way which increased my sense of entrapment. "My dear, nobody is questioning your credibility", she said to her husband, turning her face to him. "And if more people were like you these days the pharmaceutical industry would have a different reputation. Yet you say you did it for Hamlet. I suppose that is what I am questioning."

"Ah yes; that *is* the question", assented Claude with a deep sigh, enclosing her hand in his. "It is one I have often asked myself. There, somewhere, I do believe I may be guilty." *The teeth and forehead of my faults.*

There was a lull in the conversation as Lise carried a heavy soup tureen to the table. Claude poured his third glass of wine. It was almost dark outside. I was glad of the chance to digest my sense of astonishment, including that at my own romantic assumption that Hamlet's parents never quarrelled, or at least held no grievances against each other. Then, struck by a thought, I asked whether Hamlet, also, might have had suspicions about the relationship between Polack and his mother. "Oh no", laughed Gertrude quietly, giving me a mischievous glance as she passed by me to close the French doors and curtains. "In all things I am very discreet." She switched on the light over a Lowry painting over the mantlepiece and lit candles at the dinner table. We moved to it and sat down. Claude filled the wine-glasses again and we supped silently for a few minutes, musing to ourselves. *He drained the draught of Rhenish down.* Despite Gertrude's assurances, a glimmer of light now illuminated for me Hamlet's sexually rooted contempt for his parents, which had always battened on his criticism that adults assumed children understood nothing of what was going on.

At the same time I was beginning to sense something phoney in the Danes' entire milieu – Claude's "capitalistic socialism" (as Hamlet had called it), Gertrude's cultural entourage of admirers – both of which gave some substance to the origins of Hamlet's paranoia. And behind all this, my ruminations over my own marriage nagged uneasily. Gertrude's accusations about Claude "working too hard" and ignoring her had an uncannily familiar ring. Last night Beatrice had said much the same to me. Had Claude managed to tolerate a situation which I myself found intolerable?

"No, it's something I've thought about a good deal", Claude began again. "Not only recently, either. I first thought about it, Gertrude, when I was wondering about you and Antony all those years ago, and I asked myself if it was my fault." *The black and grained spots.*

"No, it was my own impatience at that time", interposed Gertrude in a conciliatory tone, sure of forgiveness, "and – frustration, about myself."

But that was not the track Claude intended to pursue. He continued, almost to himself, and with a certain quiet savagery: "Up till then I always thought, whatever my troubles and difficulties, everything will pay off in the end because my son will have been launched in life, and wherever I may have gone wrong, he will have the leisure to put it right, because he won't have had the same problems establishing himself that I had. *He had the king's word for his succession.* When I consider how my father was almost crippled by poverty in his youth – he had shoes on his feet, for the sake of family appearances, but often went for days together without a decent meal ... You understand, Dr Horacio – I'm sure you do, it's your business – that it's not only material difficulties I'm talking about. Welfare State or not, goodness is a luxury commodity if you are without security. My aim was to provide that sense of security, not only for my own family but for all my workforce."

I began to see how underneath Claude's socialist ambition (founded as it was on his own fear of poverty, and slurring over the wealth differential between himself and his workforce) there was a veiled attack on his wife for upsetting the family stability with her infidelities. Her queenliness undermined his kingliness. He drained his glass and offered more wine. Gertrude said gently,

"Hamlet can learn to be a good man if his father is a good man. That's all he needs. He doesn't need wealth."

'Ah, but that is the heart of the trouble – who is to say that I am a good man?" Claude complained (not without some hint that his wife might be to blame for his spiritual unease). "I have grave doubts about whether I am a good man. I started to have them when it became obvious that my son clearly did not view me as a good man. The first signs appeared when he was about fifteen or so. It was only the occasional snide, sarcastic comment to begin with, slipped in here and there. He'd say things like, "done any respectable drug-pushing today, Dad?" or "what have you screwed out of the Third World lately in exchange for a few sugar pills?" I was irritated of course by his self-righteousness, and above all, by his utter ignorance of the complications and frustrations involved. Yet at the same time I could see the grain of truth in his criticisms. *O limèd soul.* I knew it was only natural for a teenager to question adult values, and in a way I was proud of him for doing so. I remembered being a terrible aggravation to my father at that age. He used to say he regretted having sacrificed his own comforts all his life for the sake of having me educated, if the only use I could make of books was to fling his faults in his face. Now I suppose my sins are being visited on me." *Superfluous death.*

"No, Claude, you're too harsh on yourself", said Gertrude softly, almost in a whisper. "Those aren't sins. It's natural to have self-doubt. Your father wasn't like you, he was paranoid." But Claude hardly appeared to hear her. He refilled his glass yet again, and between mouthfuls, fondled one of the bottles on the table, turning it around. "This is our own, you know", he mumbled; "chateau-bottled."

"It's just a little house on the Garonne", Gertrude whispered aside to me, deprecatingly, "near where my grandparents lived when I was a child." She was trying to mitigate the effect of Claude's ostentation. Indeed Claude was clearly a little drunk. He began to recollect his son's childhood with a misty-eyed sentiment. *Remember me.*

"And yet", he said, "Hamlet was the most delightful child. Till he was nine or ten years old we were inseparable, he and I. His persistent plea in those days was "Daddy, can't I come too?" He used to be fascinated when I took him round the factory – never stopped asking questions! And of course we went sailing together – I used to keep a yacht at Cowes, you know, Dr Horacio – the Enterprise on the Harp is just a vestigial remnant of those days. I remember, too, when he was a toddler; he would squeal "Elephant ride, Daddy! Elephant ride!" He'd never go to bed till I'd given him an elephant ride all round the house, from the attic to the cellar." (This confirmed our associations in the analysis, I thought, with the Ghost dream in particular. *He bore me on his back a thousand times.*) "Then Gertrude would read him stories", Claude continued. "That was his programme every night. Don't you remember, *ma sourie,* that was how it was?"

Gertrude was smiling now. With a certain triumph, she recounted how she had early begun to cultivate her son's literary tastes. At the age of four, she had read him Roger Lancelyn Green's retellings of classical myths, followed by a children's *Odyssey*, "so that real literature could get into his blood from the beginning." She had done more for Hamlet, she implied, than mere elephant-rides. "I remember", she said, "even when he was in his pram, he wasn't like other babies. He never slept in the pram, he always wanted to lie on his back and gaze outwards at everything that was going on, with his bright piercing eyes – he looked so intelligent! And when old ladies came up and said "Goo goo, ga ga" to him, the way they do, he'd stare at them as if to say, what are you making those silly noises for? Can't you speak proper English? and they'd look abashed and creep away. Lise and I used to laugh." *A delicate and tender prince.*

"We were so proud of him we never wanted another child", Claude concluded.

"*You* didn't want another –"

"Nor you, Gertrude, you must admit –"

"Not at first maybe, but later I did, but then time had gone on, and it seemed too late." She spoke accusingly, distressed. *When sorrows come.*

"Well we can't always have everything we want", said her husband rather casually, as though following a deliberate policy not to pay too much attention to this irremediable sore spot. "I was the first to be disappointed in him, after all. Yet I always tried to indulge his wishes – caprices, some might call them. When he started at St Paul's, Dr Horacio, I used to send a car to pick up Nando Polack and take them both to school – but after a year or two, was that good enough? No, he had to cycle across London by bike. The underground was beneath him. So I bought him a bike. Not long after that he stopped calling me "Dad" and started to call me "Claude". Not that I minded that in itself, I knew it was the modern fashion, especially amongst the highbrow arty liberal types he was always rubbing shoulders with. At that period, I felt a bit of a fish out of water even in my own home. I was working round the clock. When I *was* at home, I saw that people were quite happy to accept my hospitality (and there were always people, God knows!). They enjoyed the good fare and entertainment they found here – but at the same time they'd turn their noses up at both business and science, which was providing it for them. Via me, that is."

Here Claude paused to drain his glass, which he refilled immediately. I could see Gertrude eyeing him anxiously – wondering, perhaps, whether to intervene. Making an effort, I suggested there was something in the climate of our age which acted against a proper appreciation and respect for science and even medicine. Claude seemed encouraged to find an ally for once:

"Yes, you would have noticed that too, Dr Horacio; my wife never believes me when I say so. But I don't think it would ever have irritated me so much if it hadn't been for Hamlet. I came to think of him as the leader in this conspiracy. Gertrude, you see, would encourage him to put in an appearance at our parties, and he'd come reluctantly at first, but then someone or other of our friends would draw him out, and he'd start entertaining the troops. He was a shy and gawky youth in those days. But he could get excitable in company – and this, I must say, always without touching a drop of alcohol. *An antic disposition.* They all applauded his antics, and I daresay cared not a jot what he was talking about. But *I* cared, because to me, it seemed he was always (beneath the thinnest of disguises) talking about me and my despicable mode of life, my hypocritical values, outdated methods, etc. You'd think I was the devil incarnate, worthy of nothing but his contempt – a monstrous fascist-racist-sexual pervert and even a miser!"

As he spoke, Claude's voice rose aggressively, spluttering to a crescendo, with traces of the paranoia which Gertrude had attributed to his own father. She had been watching him intently, and seemed to be struggling between her usual tactic of placation, and the urge to rebuff his attack on her hostess-ship. "How could we avoid socializing, with your position and the business?" she demanded. "You can hardly blame Hamlet for that – it was a necessary part of his education."

"The business!" exclaimed Claude. "It was hardly the business – how many were clients of mine? They were *your* clients – clients of your literary salon! To think, Dr Horacio –" (he appealed to me again) "that Hamlet defected from me for that crowd! Beyond the age of about ten, he never showed any curiosity in the business at all – shouldn't that have been part of his education too?"

"Antony's had difficulties with Hamlet too, you know, lately", said Gertrude, trying to divert his anger. "He said the more he praised him and tried to encourage his work, the more hostile he became, and in fact he's given up supervising him. It's a terrible shame."

"Yes, that sounds about par for the course", said Claude in a jaundiced tone. "I daresay Dr Horacio, also, has found him a bagful of trouble. When he's finished with one of us, he starts on another - isn't that the way of it? From my own point of view, things became easier for me once he left for Cambridge and we moved house - and of course, when he started seeing you, Dr Horacio."

He was calmer now, and entered his maudlin, mournful mode, the corners of his mouth drooping wearily. "It all went along with my losing interest in the business, you see, Dr Horacio – feeling that I didn't want to carry it into the next era. *The time is out of joint.* Things are changing. They always do. Who was it said you can't step into the same river twice, or even once?'

I believed it was Heraclitus. I was beginning to feel oddly detached, a receptacle-observer with only the most shadowy existence of my own, someone whose presence barely skimmed the river of their consciousness.

"Well I had the choice of either putting all my energies into the business, or of watching it slip into disorder, stalemate, corruption. I would have been quite happy to kill myself doing the former on behalf of Hamlet, but as he would hardly have appreciated the sacrifice, and I couldn't bear the idea of the latter, I chose to retire. Now I just get the odd quip from him about how I seem to be as rich as ever despite not going to work, so how was it I hadn't realized years ago that it wasn't necessary?"

Claude grimaced and set his jaw, pushing his unfinished bowl of soup away from him as Lise came round to collect them and to bring in the main course. Meanwhile Gertrude explained that in fact Claude was almost as busy as ever because he had taken on an Open University course.

"The pathos is", Claude explained, "I think I probably started even that because of Hamlet. I tried doing English and Drama first, but I could see I'd never be able to have a conversation with him about it without being ridiculed – you can't teach an old dog. So I switched to Law. And, yes, it is interesting. I'm finding it very absorbing. Very absorbing", he repeated gloomily, as he began to eat.

"I think", announced Gertrude after a moment or two, and addressing herself directly to me, "the problem is that Claude has always looked on his son in a dynastic light. Like a prince. As if it was a hereditary obligation, or necessity, for Hamlet to follow in his footsteps and take over the business, otherwise the state would collapse and there would be nothing but anarchy. *The safety and health of this whole state.* But of course it isn't like that. This is a chemical industry in the late twentieth century, not a crown in the sixteenth. We live in an age of individualism. Each person must choose what they are best fitted to do. And Hamlet's talents lie elsewhere. It is better to accept that and allow nature to take its course. After all, Claude, why should you think your life's work has been wasted just because Hamlet hasn't taken it up? Isn't the business still playing its part, now that it's with Universal? Haven't you made a contribution to humanity?"

"My dear, you at least have faith in me", said Claude wearily and resignedly. "Thank you. It's more than I have in myself. What you say about Hamlet and the business is very true. It is, I think, something I have gradually been coming to terms with for a long while. Now if I might be allowed to make an analogous point," (he said changing his tone, ponderously but with a hint of mischief) "you'll forgive me, I hope, and won't say it's just petty revenge on you and Antony."

"Well, what is it?" asked Gertrude, only half smiling.

"I think you, too, have dynastic ambitions in your way."

"Oh? – how is that?"

"Consider. Here you have been arranging a match between our only son and our – shall we say – oldest friend's only daughter. Now if that isn't dynastic, what is? Especially when the son and the oldest friend have the same kind of mind – one's just a retake of the other. Then the girl – the only daughter – is beautiful like the son's mother (and that has to be said of Ophelia, Dr Horacio). It's a heady concoction, isn't it – but has anybody considered it might be dangerous?"

"How could it be dangerous? I don't understand you, Claude", said Gertrude nervously and rather severely. Claude's speech had become blurred and fuzzy.

"Because the chemistry of their interaction may not be so predictable", he replied more aggressively. "Immature they may be, but they have to find their own way forward, even when they are as obnoxious as Hamlet or as insipid as Ophelia. It isn't up to us to thrust them together just because we think it looks poetic!"

"Come, Claude, nobody thrust them together", murmured Gertrude. She frowned and bit her lip, snuffed the candles on the dinner table and scraped off the excess wax, then relit them. "But I do see that perhaps we could have seemed too eager on their behalf, perhaps more than they could cope with", she admitted with an effort. Then, regaining her composure a little, and catching my eye to enlist my sympathy, she corrected her husband's view of Ophelia:

"And there's much more to Ophelia than meets the eye, Claude. I know her much better than you do. I've always felt a sort of responsibility towards her – no, not because of Antony – because of her not having a mother, and because of my memory of her own mother. She and I were friends, you know, Dr Horacio. It often happens, doesn't it, that motherless girls become either very brazen or very timid. Ophelia has always hidden herself away in her music. And until all this happened, her main aim in life has been to please her father. If Hamlet had turned out like that, Claude, would you have called him insipid? No, you'd just have felt satisfied that everything was going according to plan. The Polacks needed that sort of quiet relationship because they were more vulnerable, without a woman in the family. I can't express how often I've wished that Antony had married again, for the children's sake." (These last words were addressed to me, as if I could understand that Antony was another wayward child).

"Well I've wished the same myself", said Claude - without, however, any bitterness in his irony. *Methinks the lady doth protest too much.* "And what's wrong with a quiet relationship? There's enough trouble in the outside world without having to be treated as a criminal in one's own home. Does a quiet relationship have to be apologized for?"

"Of course not", said Gertrude consolingly, and a little teasingly, "just explained."

Here Lise entered with the dessert, while Claude shuffled into the kitchen to select some white wine from the fridge. Gertrude and I sat for a moment or two in embarrassed silence. I was painfully conscious of Claude's jealousy. (It reminded me, of course, of my own.) But I was shocked by his desire to humiliate Gertrude, and by her evasiveness. *The place where there is no shuffling.* I could see how Hamlet, once his infancy was past, had become a pawn in their separate dynastic ambitions. Indeed, with a struggle, they had come to recognize this, first in each other then also in themselves. Their intimacy had been undermined by Claude's scramble for money and success, and by Gertrude's queenly salon – evolved competitively when she abandoned her hope of having more children. Now (disillusioned with those years) they were attempting to adjust and repair their relationship, but it was a painful process, fraught with pitfalls. No wonder in this context the coming-together of Hamlet and Ophelia had seemed a "heady concoction". As though through them, the older generation could be recreated, saved from the decadence and corruption looming on the horizon. The Great

Erotic Hope as a means of rescuing us all from rapacity, stupidity and greed. *The roses of the state.* I realized that I, too, had fallen prey to this attitude in the analysis; I was guilty of similarly pressurizing Hamlet.

Impelled in some way by Gertrude's embarrassed look of appeal, I confessed something of my sense of analytic failure to the Danes. They had, after all, been very open with me about their own problems. *Give them good watch, Horatio.* But they seemed rather nonplussed at the depth of my concern. Claude repeated that in his view Hamlet was much better, and Gertrude gazed intensely at me with her liquid brown eyes and said softly and reassuringly that I was "far too modest". I knew they had not really expected much of me or the analysis. Their contact with the profession was a social one, and they had no idea or interest in the traumas or delicate handling it entailed. I was an employee who had done his duty; no blame could attach to me. My apology was just modesty. Indeed, in Gertrude's eyes, it was really a form of homage to her personally, humbling myself before her attractiveness.

By coffee and brandy Claude and Gertrude had become more relaxed and harmonious. I no longer felt I was required to take sides in their fencing match. The triangular tension between us was defused, and I almost felt a temporary inmate of their little circle. Gertrude kissed Lise and sent her to bed. "She's the only one left', she explained. "We used to have lots of staff but now they've all gone, thank God; we don't need anyone but ourselves. Lise is family. The house is so peaceful."

I asked a question or two about Hamlet's friends, and Gertrude replied that Nando was turning out to be "untrustworthy": "Heaven knows what shifty deals he and that other fellow – what's his name, Forte something – concoct between them in the City. *A list of lawless resolutes.* His social behaviour is impeccable, of course. But his charm is of a cold type. The English Gentleman is not what he used to be. You complain about your own son, Claude, but you don't realize how lucky you are. And I'm sure he'll settle down eventually, won't he, Dr Horacio?"

Before the evening concluded, however, the conversation returned to the relationship between Hamlet and Ophelia and to Hamlet's play production.

"It was very clever, of course", said Claude, "and I realize that's the modern way, to introduce all sorts of extraneous bits and pieces to liven it up. But to my mind, it wasn't ideal for those two youngsters to be having a type of filmstar affair on the stage – that never works, does it. I'm not surprised they split up, quite apart from the pregnancy business." *Your father is much offended.*

"Well I didn't think it was so clever anyway", said Gertrude. "It was done for cheap laughs, like so many productions these days. *A Midsummer Night's Dream* is funny enough in itself without all that jazz and slapstick added to it. Hamlet should have known better. I could have smacked him afterwards, he gave me such an insolent look." *You answer with an idle tongue.*

"If you're not careful you'll find Hamlet disappoints your literary ambitions for him, just as he disappointed my industrial ones", warned Claude. Yet again, I found myself acutely aware of his jealousy, and how this was bound up with the feeling that his son had been kidnapped into the camp of the enemy, run by his wife with her literary admirers – leaving him in the position of a mere stepfather. Hamlet's uncle-father indeed.

"No, I have confidence in him after all", stated the queen his mother firmly. "He was in a mess, that's why. Have I ever denied he was in a mess? What can you expect after the collapse of his first serious love affair?" (She seemed to temporarily ignore the possibility that the "mess" caused the collapse, rather than vice versa.)

"Tell me, Dr Horacio", Claude suddenly turned to me with a newly inquiring tone. "What is your professional assessment of Hamlet's talents? I mean as a writer, a poet - after all, that's what we all really expect him to become, something creative. I know what my wife thinks; and myself, I'm not qualified to have any opinion on the matter. It's suddenly struck me: is he genuinely talented, or is he just one of those clever dicks who switch on as soon as they've got an audience? And then complain that everybody's watching them. What do you think?"

I thought (privately) that in my most pessimistic moments my own worst fears about Hamlet had indeed taken that form. But to counterbalance them I had the evidence of his richly imaginative dream-life; and in my heart's core I "believed" that somewhere there was talent. I explained to his father that from a literary point of view it would be better to ask somebody like Professor Polack, who knew his work. An analyst only sees potentialities.

"Ah well, we'll just have to wait and see", said Claude.

He offered to drive me home when I confessed that I had come on foot that evening; but I preferred to escape over the now deserted Heath in the cool night air, open to scudding clouds and watery starlight that temporarily swept the contagion from my soul.

CHAPTER NINE

Ophelia at Colonus

> **Ophelia**: But good my brother,
> Do not, as some ungracious pastors do,
> Show me the steep and thorny way to heaven,
> Whiles like a puff'd and reckless libertine
> Himself the primrose path of dalliance treads,
> And recks not his own rede. (I. iii. 45-51)

Horacio's consultation with Ophelia confirms her disturbing effect upon Hamlet and makes clear his ignorance of her character. Still Horacio has not fathomed the completeness of his own mistake.

By now my own newly recognized loneliness was beginning to bite. Meeting Hamlet's parents had done nothing to alleviate that; in fact it had exacerbated it. I suspected, though did not yet understand, that it was bound up in some vaguely non-analytic way with Hamlet's unconcluded analysis. And I was still hungry for more information. This was why, when Ophelia Polack contacted me at the end of term asking for a consultation, I agreed to see her myself rather than referring her to someone else. It was not my normal practice, but these circumstances, I told myself (as with the Danes), were unusual. I almost felt that I needed to see her: that it was owed to me. And since learning of her miscarriage, a certain ambivalence towards her which I had noticed in myself had been replaced by a revival of curiosity.

As I waited for her to arrive, I realized that the question I really wanted to have answered about Ophelia was, could she possibly be as beautiful as Hamlet had led me to believe? After all, beauty in the eyes of a nineteen-year-old boy could well mean no more than fashionability, and I prepared myself to be disappointed. But when I saw Ophelia in the waiting room I too was impressed. She was dressed quirkily in a long ragged-edged green skirt, tight T shirt, and strange patched and brocaded sleeveless jacket. But she moved with a natural grace the envy of finishing schools, and her face shone out of a Botticelli painting, with a delicate long nose tapering straight between her grey eyes, and bronze-blonde hair reaching half-way down her back.

"Miss Polack?" I nodded, inviting her in to the consulting room.

"It's all right, please call me Ophelia", she said as she entered and sat down. "I know you've been seeing Hamlet. It was his mother who gave me your address. I asked her, because I need to have some objective advice. My father doesn't know – I can't tell him anything any more, he only worries and gets upset. In hospital there was Paulina, I could talk to her – I expect you know about Paulina?"

I saw that Ophelia expected me both to know all about her and to be able to offer her objective advice. She spoke with more self-assurance than I had expected, and slightly hurriedly, as though she believed she had to cram an enormous amount into our limited time. She continued:

"Well, Paulina was the nurse on our ward and I could tell her things I couldn't tell Gertrude, because she's Hamlet's mother and besides has known me since childhood – she's too involved."

She hesitated as though these "things" were gathering massively in her mind and all about to demand formulation simultaneously.

"Do you know about my father and me, and Hamlet's family and mine?" she asked, as though there might be a short-cut if she could rely on what I knew already. All these people "knowing about" each other, yet again, without ever knowing themselves, I thought. *Lord we know what we are, but know not what we may be.* But I asked her, of course, to tell her story in her own words.

"Well when we were children", she began, "our families were very close and we saw a lot of each other. We used to live in the same road, and at first my father lived in the Danes' house; that was when my mother was alive – she and Gertrude had been at the Sorbonne together and that was why, when my father came over during the war, my parents had the top floor of their house. We only moved to Cambridge when Daddy got the professorship, and even then Nando – that's my brother – stayed at school in London as a boarder. He and Hamlet went to the same school and Daddy didn't want to move him. You see, our mother died when I was three. You know that of course. My brother was five. I don't remember her at all and I don't believe Nando does either, except from photographs and what Daddy has told us. In the photos Daddy was already bald, and much skinnier than he is now. Mother looks very like Nando. And Daddy has always had a sort of reverential attitude to her, almost standing in awe of her memory. He always says it was a miracle the way she smuggled him across the continent during the war.

"I know other people used to ask him why he didn't marry again. I used to think when I was a girl, that they were ignorant, and it showed how noble and strong-minded Daddy was. He put all his energies into me and Nando (apart from his work of course, he's always been fanatical about that.) You see, he felt he had to be father and mother to us both; it was like a vocation for him, to see that we never missed out. Maybe more like a religion. He has never been religious in any other way, though of course he is Jewish; but we aren't, because mother wasn't. Also, he doesn't really feel English himself – I know that. He's taken out British citizenship, and he's a professor of English, but he still feels a foreigner. It's something I almost can't understand, because of course I feel English through and through.

"I remember when this first struck me. It was one evening a long time ago, when we still lived in London – the three of us – and we watched a programme on TV about the Holocaust. Nando asked Daddy if that was what happened to his relatives – which means, in a way, *our* relatives. At the end Daddy switched off the TV and swivelled his chair to face us (he always sat in this huge, high-backed revolving leather chair – he still does). He told us he thought the best inheritance he could ever give us was an English education, and how in his view this small island led the world because of its literature and its ideas of justice and morality." *A vision of the island.*

"Then he swivelled away as if he wanted to hide his face from us. The room was dark with the TV off. Nando got up and stomped out. I remember feeling terribly uncomfortable, because I'd never seen Daddy like that, and I didn't really understand what he was talking about. But later I realized that he had particular expectations of Englishness that were to do with his being a foreigner. And how it was a bit like his attitude to our mother, or the memory of our mother."

Here Ophelia paused and said perhaps she was going off the point. I assured her she wasn't, and she said, "You're not really English either, are you?" I smiled to myself when she said this (remembering the devout English correctness of my grandfather, the rabbi); but I saw that she was introducing herself to me as an alternative version of her father. I wondered what had happened between them, and asked her to continue to describe her present relationship with him.

"That's the trouble – it's completely changed", she lamented. "Now it's almost as if I were *his* mother. And it's all Hamlet's fault."

She paused again, a little provocatively, as if to test my reaction and see whether I would take sides on this issue. But when I just grunted questioningly, she continued:

"Ever since Hamlet seemed to turn against him, and went all cold and sarcastic, I've noticed this change in Daddy. You see – it's because of Nando as well. It only became clear to me when I was in hospital, that Daddy finds Nando a disappointment. They're not the same type at all, of course – just not interested in the same things. Nando never even wanted to go to university – he went straight into the City. And Daddy can't bear it when things don't turn out his way. So when Hamlet came along it was as though he'd found an adopted son, the son he always really wanted – clever and full of ideas, and mad about English literature. They had a fantastic relationship at first. And after a while, when I started going out with Hamlet, I began to feel that it was *me* keeping them together, too. I felt sort of – proud and important. Does that sound stupid and arrogant to you?" (she asked anxiously), and then, "terribly babyish, then?"

Again I said no, it made sense.

"It was a bit like the first time I sang a solo with the choir in King's Chapel when I was still at school", she explained.

In what way was it like that? I asked.

"It was partly the glory of course – knowing I could do it in front of everyone – but it was also that I felt I was doing something for Daddy, because he wanted it. *My father's behest.* That's a lousy reason, isn't it?"

Not lousy, I said, just not sufficient.

"But then", she continued, "I got pregnant and everything changed. Before that, I never even asked myself if I liked Hamlet or not, for himself that is. I suppose I was kind of amazed at first that he liked *me*. I did wonder, if it hadn't been for my father, would he ever have noticed me? I knew all about him, of course, because in the first year he was into everything – all the protests, sit-ins, plays and things too. Though he never said a word to me all that year. But mainly I knew about him from Daddy, who was his Director of Studies. Daddy said he was the best student he'd ever had. It was Hamlet who got Daddy to organize the acting workshop on Gawain and the Green Knight, and Daddy decided to do it every year, all in Middle English. I was the lady with the belt in that, because I could play the mandolin. That was when Hamlet noticed me. It was strange because even though we knew each other from childhood, we pretended we didn't – it was like another existence. Well *I* pretended anyway. I thought Hamlet was so incredibly busy being such a big noise, he probably didn't even know who I was."

Possibly, I suggested, she had actually *dis*liked him?

"Oh no, it wasn't that", she said quickly. "I never disliked him, even when I thought he'd gone mad and didn't know what he was saying. I just took it that he was living on a different plane from me. And I had a sort of boyfriend, but that was for safety's sake – after all, I grew up in Cambridge and I knew you had to be some sort of Valkyrie to survive the university meat markets (that's what they call the freshers' parties). Daddy was dead keen that I should go to Cambridge. I had a secret wish to go to the Royal Academy in London, but I never told him that. Daddy said Cambridge was like Colonus to Athens – the gateway to the heart of English civilization. So as soon as I knew I'd got in, I became desperate to lose my virginity." *The maid that never departed more.*

Her tone became harder and a little defiant when she said this, as if testing to see whether I was shocked.

"And I did lose it", she continued, "the summer before going up, with this oafish hippy character at a pop festival in Grantchester meadows. I loathed every second of it but I was really triumphant afterwards; I thought, I've done it – I've got rid of it! Then I felt kind of armoured, and I knew I could face anything, even the University. I did think, if Daddy only knew ... but of course he had no idea, thank God. Now *you* know, Dr Horacio, and you'll see how horrible I am. I'm only telling you all this because I know that as a psychoanalyst you can't get a proper picture of someone without knowing about their sexual history."

I said she seemed regretful that her first sexual experience had been a cold one.

"Yes, that was it", she said, sounding relieved; "and I know it wasn't like that for my friend Rosalind, for example. Even at school she could always string along crowds of men. I don't mean she was a tease; she just didn't have the same inhibitions as me. It was personality, not looks – I know I'm prettier than she is. Somehow she knew how to organize her life so she only had sex for enjoyment, not for –" (she hesitated).

"Armament?" I repeated, wondering to what extent this was a defence against the impact of her beauty.

"Sort of", she said confusedly, "that time, anyway. It was different with Hamlet. There were one or two disasters at the beginning, like the first time there was blood all over the college mattress because it was the middle of my period, but that was just as well since he didn't have a condom, and the next time he kept fumbling with the wretched thing and said he hated them, but it was really only his vanity that was upset. In fact all that term I think I was on a kind of a high, I couldn't think about anything else – except sex, and the Play, and him. And I couldn't get over the fact that he'd chosen me, rather than Ros or any of the others – I knew quite a few people fancied him. *Th'observed of all observers.* Yes", she said, as if something had become clarified, "I had all those emotions mixed up, at the same time. That's why I couldn't imagine talking to my father or Gertrude about it – you could see the only question at the back of their minds would be: do you love him, or don't you?"

And that, it was evident, she didn't know how to answer, even now. I asked to what extent she believed the Play had confused their relationship?

"Oh – it did, I suppose – it got too glamorous, too exciting, it wasn't quite real. It was like drugs in a way. I can see that now. But perhaps I never would have realized it if it hadn't been for getting pregnant. That, and the miscarriage. Suddenly everything crashed down with a bump. *Quite, quite down.* Hamlet seemed to change overnight, I could hardly recognize him. I couldn't even *tell* him; every time I tried it was like banging my head on a brick wall. The way he spoke to me – I almost thought he was mad. You know – really psychotic. That was the first time I asked myself, what did I really feel about him, as a person – not just about being Hamlet's girlfriend in front of everybody else, or sex and how many marks out of ten it got each time. And I couldn't tell if I hated him or hated myself."

I asked in what way she had hated herself?

"It was really that I was furious with myself, for being such a stupid little fool. The night it happened, I didn't notice he wasn't using a condom till afterwards -" (So, I thought, there was something concrete behind Hamlet's sanctimonious confusion.) "Then he said it was bound to be all right because my period was due in a few days anyway. I couldn't believe it when my period never came. I thought that only happened to ignorant little schoolgirls. I felt cold with fear, because I knew it would have to be aborted. *Conception is a blessing, but as your daughter may conceive...* That made me angry, too – I thought, why should I let that be done to *my* body, just because of him?"

Why she was so sure the baby would have to be aborted?

"That was it – I just couldn't imagine having a baby, that was mine. It wasn't possible. Gertrude kept talking about 'the baby'. She tried to persuade me to keep it. You'd think it was her own, she was so keen – she had plans for its room, and having Lise help to look after it – Hamlet's nanny. And after I'd had that talk with her, I remembered something that happened a long time ago, in that other life, when we lived in London and saw so much of the Danes. I don't know why, but it flashed vividly into my mind.

"It was one winter when there was lots of snow, especially in Hampstead because of the hills, and it lasted for weeks, which was so unusual of course. Everybody moaned about it but as children we thought it was paradise. I must have been eleven or twelve at the time – it was the year before we moved to Cambridge. And I remember bitterly that Daddy wouldn't let me have a toboggan of my own – he thought it was a waste of money, since we hardly ever got snow like that, and I could easily share Nando's, it was big enough for two – in fact he thought it was better if Nando did the steering for both of us. So I used to take a tea-tray for the times when Nando wouldn't let me have a go, which was often. Hamlet had his own toboggan of course, and it was the best type – wooden slats with metal runners. Sometimes Hamlet let me go on his, but mostly he and Nando were obsessed with racing each other down the hill, which meant I couldn't go on either and had to use the tea-tray. Anyway – on the Sunday morning which looked as if it might be the last before the snow melted – we set off early for the Heath. You know there's this steep valley at the side of West Heath Lane. *Show me the steep and thorny way.* We'd been there till dark the day before, with hundreds of other people. This time we were the first; the place was empty. Hamlet and Nando started discussing where they were going to run their first race, as usual. I felt fed up and said I wanted to have a go, on my own, and Nando said – as usual – "Just hold on a minute, Phely, you can have a go later." I knew it was probably the last day, and there was school tomorrow, and suddenly I was filled with absolute fury. I grabbed the strings of the toboggan off him and shrieked at the top of my voice, "Give it to me, you bugger! I hate you! And I *will* go first!" He was so astonished, he started sniggering; and Hamlet just stared at me as if I was mad.

"What none of us had noticed was that the main run was in a lethal condition, because so many people had been on it the day before and there was no fresh snow; it was worn into steep humps and covered in a sheet of ice. The toboggan bounced from one hump to the next at breakneck speed, and eventually I was thrown off and broke my arm. The toboggan was in splinters. Hamlet went to fetch Daddy, who was furious with Nando. He said he'd be grounded at home for a month with no pocket money. I came back from hospital with my arm in plaster, feeling very virtuous and important, and Nando spent the next week glowering and hissing at me.

"I suppose I remembered that because it was the only other time I'd been in hospital. But it made me feel terrified of the abortion. It was the operation I was scared of, Dr Horacio, not losing the baby. I thought I couldn't go through with it. The next night I woke up lying in a pool of blood. For a minute I thought I was dying. Then I realized, it had miscarried. It should have been the best way out of it all for me: I didn't want the baby and I didn't want the abortion. But it wasn't, it was the beginning of a nightmare. I had terrible dreams; I wandered about not knowing what I was doing. I felt full of guilt, as if I must have somehow caused the miscarriage by having bad thoughts about the baby and not wanting it. *Summoned like a guilty thing.* At the same time I believed there was something wrong with me and I would never be able to have a child. Or that between us, Hamlet and I had created a monster and it was a judgement on our lousy relationship. *Be damned if I let this monster live.* Do you understand what I mean?" she asked with a certain desperation.

Yes, I said, I understood. Possibly her feeling of guilt related also to her description of "getting rid of her virginity", as though she had somehow "got rid of" the baby in the same way.

"That night", she said, "I had a dream where *my mother's coffin was lying across the top of the wardrobe in our old flat in Hampstead, and I knew it was going to slip off and crash unless I could press the right spot on the door which would stop it – and I couldn't find the right place.*"

So it crashed? I asked, and she confirmed it. It was also, of course, like the toboggan incident, when she had felt both bullied by the boys and, at the same time, to blame herself in more complex ways – lack of judgement (not "noticing" the conditions, as with the condom), startling her brother then blaming him, instead of earlier explaining the situation about the toboggans clearly to her father. In the same way she had not told her father she really wanted to go to the Royal Academy, thus depriving him of the chance to help her pursue her own desires, instead of obediently shadowing his. *I shall obey, my lord.*

"But his heart was set on me going to Cambridge!" she exclaimed, astonished. Perhaps, I pointed out, his heart was even more set on *her*. He might have liked to know what she wanted. This might have given him pleasure greater than if she merely fulfilled his own wishes. But she had been so anxious to avoid a battle with him that she had not given him the opportunity.

At this point Ophelia burst into tears. Probably, I thought, she had never been spoken to so severely in her life. The Professor, I imagined, could not stand confrontations either. With some violent sobs of relief, which soon came to an end, she told me that now she knew why she had slit her wrists. "It was to get away from him because I couldn't talk to him. There was no other way I could tell him I needed to be in hospital. As soon as I got there I felt better, immediately – safe and shut away. Paulina helped about the miscarriage, and so in a funny way did the other girls. Most of them had anorexia, and were younger than me. I could see they were revolted by the idea of developing sexually, and I vaguely remembered that as something I had got over, though I never had anorexia as an illness.

For the first time I felt like an older sister. I felt I had a sort of responsibility to show them a hopeful example. When Gertrude came to visit me, we didn't talk about Hamlet, we talked about the other girls, and I got on much better with her."

Perhaps, I suggested, amongst women both older and younger than herself, she had managed to re-establish contact with her own femininity, in terms of being mothered and also of feeling that she might one day be able to be a mother, starting by discovering her older-sister feelings.

"Yes", she said, "I even felt strong enough to tell my friend Ros to fuck off when she came in to say I'd only done it to get him to marry me – and that then I had a breakdown because he wouldn't. I told her she was jealous of the whole thing – even the breakdown. Still I hated her afterwards. But it put things in perspective."

In what way? I asked – explaining the humiliation?

"Maybe, I don't know", she said (not really considering this aspect). "It made me concentrate on what was important – because after she had gone it came to me that the person I was really worrying about, more than the girls, was my father."

She was worried about the effect her breakdown had had on him?

"Even before that. I told you Hamlet was being horrible to him. And I'd noticed Daddy was kind of down, even while we were doing the Play – noticed it unconsciously, but I just didn't think about it, I was so swept up in the Play. In hospital, though, I thought about it a lot. I don't know why Hamlet turned against him. But it was obvious to everyone that he had – Gildstein noticed and so did other people. He was never actually rude to him, just poisonous and sarcastic in the way which only he can be – and all for no reason at all. Of course Daddy turned him over to a new supervisor, but that wasn't the point. The fact is, he was deeply hurt by Hamlet's behaviour. He told me about it just after I came out of hospital. I expect he didn't want to say anything till he thought I was better. He was sitting in his old leather swivel chair in his study, silhouetted against the window at the end (the rest of the room is completely book-lined). *Furnished with volumes prized above his dukedom.*

"'My dear child', he began, "everything I've ever done has been with you in mind – your prosperity and future happiness. *I have done nothing but in care of thee, my daughter.* Yes. And your brother, of course. It was not simply my duty to your dear mother but my pleasure, as you know. Now you're a grown woman yourself, and you've pulled through a difficult time, I can talk to you a little about myself. Everything Hamlet says about me is true. It's true that I am past my prime, I've been teaching in the same old way for years and I am stuck in a rut. *Rapt in secret studies.* My reputation will soon start to fade, and the English faculty needs young blood, new stars. But where are they to be found? In the Rosenfelds and Gildsteins of this world? Surely I must be forgiven for hoping that Hamlet, or somebody like Hamlet, would fulfil this role. Who could be in a better position than me to promote him and advance his career? Yet what does he do but stab me in the ribs? Fashions in literary interpretation – they all fade away, and myself amongst them; I have no illusions of my immortality. *The cloud-capp'd towers, the gorgeous palaces.* But the spirit of literature lives on, must live on.

"'I hope you won't mind my mentioning Hamlet, my dear, now that you've got over him.'" (I noticed that Ophelia's voice trembled slightly when she conveyed this, but she made no comment, and continued with her father's lament.) "'I realize that I'm getting old, and susceptible to wish-fulfilment. And that was a bright wish while it lasted; I really believed, and so did the Danes, that you and Hamlet were ideally matched. Don't be unhappy about him – you'll find somebody else to love, you've got your whole life ahead of you. In ten years' time you'll meet unexpectedly somewhere and shake hands and be the best of friends. No, I'm the one who has suffered a permanent wound. My horizons are closing in.

"'What high hopes I had of him at first! I remember, when he came up for interview, his tongue-in-cheek defiance about the association between our families. He said he applied to Christ's only because Milton went there, and he'd stayed at St Paul's for the same reason, not because it was the family crypt. He said it with a charming grin, daring me to disbelieve him, and I thought: we can work together. He genuinely loved Milton.

Another time when he wrote his essay on wordgames and the demise of the image in *Samson Agonistes* – and it was a very lively argument, skin-tight to the text, if a bit over the top ideologically – I asked him if he was becoming a structuralist? and he replied in his satirical way: "A piss on ists – I'd rather have my balls cut off than be any kind of an ist, I'm not even an anarchist!" And then he added, looking hard at me: "After all, it was Milton who said you should never subscribe slave to ideologies, wasn't it?" Yes, Ophelia, I really thought Hamlet was a man after my own heart. His youthful iconoclasm would be just the right leavening agent for my own wide-ranging scholarship. Do you know, my dear, they used to call me Spellbinder?' *Held in this bare island by your spell.*

"And Daddy went on in this way for about two hours, after I got home from hospital. Almost every day now he says something along the same lines. It made me feel very strange. Both distant from him, and close to him. I could see, though, that the balance of our relationship had changed. Now I feel older than him, because I can see he *is* getting old, and he doesn't enjoy the fray any more (as he used to call it). Perhaps it was true that he suffered more from Hamlet's unpredictability than I did. He had expectations of Hamlet; but I was somehow part of the expectation, caught up in it. I couldn't see outside it."

I asked if her father talking about Hamlet had helped her to clarify her own feelings?

"It was strange, because at first I was almost angry that he talked about Hamlet as if it was so easy for me to 'get over it', and then the book could be shut for ever. But then I found I was actually hoping he'd say more about Hamlet and what he was like in supervisions. It was like when he used to tell us stories before going to bed. Daddy never read books to us, he always told stories out of his head, from books he knew so well that they were part of him. I could match up things he said about Hamlet with other things in my memory that I somehow never paid attention to when they happened. As if piecing together a story – I could say yes, that's what he was like. For example, I remember the time when he was sitting in front of the gas fire in his room and he started laughing and reading a bit out of his book; it was the letters of Keats. He held his pencil up and put his foot on the fender and said that perhaps that was the position John Keats was sitting in, when he wondered what was the position Shakespeare sat in when he began 'To be or not to be'. He seemed to think that was hilariously funny – it was to do with what Keats had written about reading Shakespeare. But in some strange way it seemed to be about *us*, and it made me laugh too – I felt so lighthearted, you know, *happy*."

I pointed out to Ophelia that she said this almost as if it were a revelation that there really was such a thing as happiness to be had. She sounded a little taken aback, as though I might be misunderstanding the main import of her speech.

"It's just that, looking back on it, those were the best times', she explained, "nothing to do with the Play. But I can only look back at all because I know it's all over. It's the one thing I can be certain of. Have I got time to tell you one more thing? You know what made me decide to get in touch with you? It was when I bumped into Hamlet for the first time since all this happened. It was in the Market. I saw he was looking miserable, and I wanted to say it was my fault too, but I couldn't. I was afraid he might explode. I still didn't trust his temper. So you see how it is", she said with a note of finality.

And indeed, with frustration, I saw how it was, and saw my helplessness to do anything about it. Ophelia had one more question for me before she left:

"Tell me, Dr Horacio – was it really my fault? I'm worried I might be a complete bitch. What do you really think?"

It was not, of course, a question which required an answer. I saw that Ophelia had come to me for absolution, with regard to her mental disturbance after the miscarriage, and also troubled by the effect this had had on her father and to some extent on Hamlet. The act of confession was what she wanted, rather than any more specific aid; and doubtless, had her father not become so dependent on her, she would have confided in him. Probably she had been accustomed to do so throughout her life. And she, at least, had learned from her experience of the past year. Nevertheless I offered, should she wish it, to arrange for her to see someone therapeutically on a regular basis. I explained that

I could not see her myself since I was still hoping that Hamlet would return to his analysis at some point. She never did take up this offer, however, and it was some years before I had news of her again.

After she had gone, as I had a cancellation, I estimated I had time for a brisk walk across the Vale of Health to the sloping, soothing lawns of Kenwood House and back. Hamlet's desertion, Ophelia's beauty, and Beatrice's alienation, were ringing the changes in my mind, confirming my confusion and vague sense of guilt. *The understanding begins to swell.* Nothing, however, led me to any soothing conclusions, or even to any clarification of thought. *The approaching tide will shortly fill the reasonable shore that now lies foul and muddy.*

CHAPTER TEN

Becoming Fortinbras

> **Hamlet**: I lov'd Ophelia. Forty thousand brothers
> Could not with all their quantity of love
> Make up my sum ...
> Woo'd weep, woo't fight, woo't fast, woo't tear thyself,
> Woo't drink up eisel, eat a crocodile?
> I'll do it. Dost come here to whine,
> To outface me with leaping in her grave? (V. i. 264-73)

Horacio is bitterly disappointed by Hamlet on his return eight years later, after having followed the Forte road to intellectual yuppydom, and begins to understand his own mismanagement of the analysis.

My further acquaintance with the Danes and Polacks left me with mixed feelings. I was more conscious than ever of the seductiveness of his home environment, this nest of sensitive and cultured opportunity in which no expense was spared. Polack too, in his way, was an agent or offshoot from this. But I remembered Hamlet saying nobody wanted "a feller with a social disease". I was now in a position to understand better the social aspects of the disease by which both their houses were plagued – the confusion over status and privilege, the loss of identity, fear of being overwhelmed by a new dark age of cynicism and greed, and guilt at personal failings or past mistakes which may have helped to induce it. This was, to some extent, the spirit of the age, pressing on all of us. *The time was out of joint.* But I was disillusioned by the degree to which Claude and Gertrude had fallen prey to it, and I regretted not having given due weight to Hamlet's own adolescent struggle, his fight against it. This was the fault of my own blindness, my idealization of his princely origins.

And now, the impact of Ophelia's beauty widened my perspective on the nature of this struggle. Before meeting her myself, I had suspected her beauty was primarily an aspect of Hamlet's own arrogance, a label to make her match his own princely status. I understood now that it was a genuine source of emotional turbulence. I also saw how little Hamlet knew her, how his curiosity had somehow stopped at the barrier of beauty. The grandiosity of her father (not unlike Claude's) now became evident. But Ophelia showed herself to have enough spirited potential to emerge from her meek, flat obedience, while respecting his vulnerability.

Indeed the meeting with Ophelia remained a romantic glow at the back of my mind, a symbol of hope over the following years. During this period I maintained occasional social contact with the Danes, and learned of Ophelia's marriage. This did not affect the idea I had that in some way she represented the key to Hamlet's rejuvenation and the resuscitation of his abortive analysis. My hopes of course lay as much in analysis as in marriage, and I had been disappointed that Ophelia had never asked me for a referral. It was eight years before I heard from Hamlet again, and all the while I had been awaiting his return. It was a bad time in my own life. I had gradually come to accept the irretrievable breakdown of my relationship with my wife, although until recently we still lived together. My daughters were causing me some anxiety, and the bitterness of Beatrice's long-expected departure still stung. In a strange way I seemed to believe that I could not make proper headway with my own problems until I understood the mystery of Hamlet and his departure, which had taken such a hold on my mind.

Then in November 1981, I suddenly received a request from Hamlet for an appointment. It was shortly after the death of his father.

I had not seen him during those eight years, but his progress in life was not unknown to me. In fact I had observed his career with some concern. For the last three or four years he had been writing a regular column for *The Dictator*, that organ of the thinking classes whose large leafy pages I allowed (in common with everybody else) to float freely above and about me on Sunday afternoons in the garden, the lounging chair locking both mind and body in a state of idle stupefaction which was given a nightmare quality by the strange juxtaposition of images in one's head: female buttocks superimposed on pot-bellied children served up as haute cuisine; sofa beds and gigantic tin-openers slicing brown-skinned youths to pieces in full colour. There was, indeed, a variety of entertainments - something for every bit of the mindlessness. Jumbled into a sickly haze after lunch, the conscience of consumerism rotated grumblingly through one's bowels.

Amidst the haze I could not help noticing, and from time to time glancing through, Hamlet's contributions. They gave me no pleasure, and I never pursued further the longer articles or books which he was doubtless also producing for the industry of the printed word. His was a "serious" column, designed for the conscience side of the mindlessness, and flirting occasionally with the cultural side. He wrote on subjects ranging from politics in South America to ecology and the consumerisation of conscience. His research seemed impeccable and his conclusions worthy. But it pained me to suspect that his "youthful iconoclasm" (as Professor Polack had termed it) might be merging into step-ahead fashionability; as soon as a topic became fashionable, he dropped it and took up the one in advance. If this was his idiosyncratic view of the status he wished to preserve, it was a far cry from his early passionate interest in literature. Occasionally, also, he printed a poem of his own. This would usually be about the inevitable failure of yet another inadequate and meaningless relationship, written with a certain facile, facetious flair. To my mind, their literary merit seemed negligible, and they even lacked the vitality of the one or two coarse juvenile verses which had come to my attention during his analysis.

Consequently, when he asked to see me again, amongst the mixed emotions which sprung up in me was a revived hope that perhaps he was dissatisfied with his present mode of life.

He seemed pleased to see me when he entered, looking dapper, dark and handsome and (apart from his slighter build) very much more like his father than formerly, with the same ironic, melancholy mouth, and cropped hair that had even become slightly wavy.

"Hail, Dr Horacio, well met after this many a day", he said debonairly, shaking hands but allowing his glance to slip past mine and rove quickly over the room to detect any changes. "Same old carpet", he added in the same artificially jovial tone, and then before lying down he handed me a glossy paperback, saying "My latest book – I bet you haven't read it yet. It's called *Where Are We Now?*"

With distaste I placed this volume on the side-table and waited for him to begin.

"I expect you know, my father died two months ago?" *Imperious Caesar, dead and turn'd to clay.*

Yes, I said; I was sorry.

"I was sorry too. I was sorry I'd never really let him into my life again. And now it's too late. When he died, I imagined you telling me I'd treated him badly. I remember his expression when I refused to let him give me the deposit for a house, a couple of years ago. 'Keep the Danegeld, Dad', I said – it was a joke, that's what I used to call my pocket-money. I remember how his face fell. It was the first time I'd called him Dad for years, too."

And now, I said, he regretted his ingratitude.

"You see", said Hamlet defensively, "I thought he'd understand – after all, when he was my age he must have wanted to prove himself too. That's why I never accepted any money from him from the time I left University."

Whereas now, I presumed, he had accepted it all. I wondered whether it was indeed his father's death that was the stimulus for his coming to see me – his feelings of guilt at a relationship that had never been repaired, made worse by the burden of financial inheritance.

"It's true I feel guilty", he admitted, "but I don't give a damn about the money one way or the other. It's the relationship. I've come to see you because I know you're not affected by the sort of hypersensitivities which suspend sound judgment and make people see my motives in the wrong light. Perhaps you'll believe me, when I tell you I went to see Professor Polack last week – for the first time since I left Cambridge."

Had Professor Polack regarded him in the wrong light, then? *My son in the ooze is bedded.*

"Not now, no – in fact he was really pleased to see me. That's the point; I regretted not going before. I suppose I went to somehow make up for not seeing my father more."

Perhaps, I suggested, he had come to see me for the same reason. He rejected this adamantly: "Oh no, Dr Horacio, it's quite different. Not only is Polly physically frail, he's out of touch – even though in some ways his mind's as sharp as a pin. I guess it was good to see him because it made a refreshing change from the real world."

The real world? I queried.

"The pressures of the system – you'll see when you read my book, they're all exposed in it" (*where we are now*, I reminded myself). "You'll see how it is that Gildstein's ended up running a pension fund racket, and Rosenfeld's a consultant for health service management, and Nando is in Bahrein screwing money out of the Arabs. While Forte, of course, has got a special government commission to sell arms on all sides." *A yeasty collection.*

And what about Hamlet himself – *now*? I demanded rather testily.

"Well I reckon I'm coming to the end of the road with *The Dictator*", he announced (at which my spirits brightened). "It was good while it lasted – helped me maintain my independence. I never had to sell my soul for yuppy lucre. But I'm getting sick of it. I've decided I need to change my lifestyle, it's blocking my creativity. On *The Dictator* there's nobody whose main preoccupation isn't whose arse they are going to lick or be licked by next. It's as bad as any parochial rag from that point of view. You remember the abominable Mrs Forte?" (he spoke confidentially, humorously, as if this were a joke we could share); "she got me a job on it in the first place. After Cambridge, you see, I knew I had to get away somewhere really different or I'd die of claustrophobia – I hated my last year there, and I could see academic English was finished. *The bubbles are out.* So I told the paper – on impulse – that I wanted to go to Argentina; and I went there, then to Nicaragua, then Chile." *I sat me down, devised a new commission, wrote it fair.*

He recounted the year or two he had spent reporting from South America and how he had come to the conclusion it wasn't really his scene and decided to concentrate on ecological issues. "Those were on a scale I felt I could do something about. Did you read my investigations of the dioxin disaster at Seveso, and the St Rocher scandal? Those big chemical conglomerates are shit. But I never attacked Universal, because of my father. I knew he'd have taken it personally. Though they're no better than the others. So you see – I did spare some thought for his feelings, even when I had to establish myself."

I recognized that phrase "establish myself" from his father. Hamlet seemed unaware of how his own grandiosity, in its sanctimonious ecological form, paralleled that of his father with his benign socialist patriarchy. He had always been vulnerable to patronisation (despite his contempt for it); and I blamed myself for the time I had wasted on moral lecturing, which had done nothing but confirm his sanctimony, as appeared now in his journalism.

"But now I need a change of scene", he pointed out. "Now I'm financially independent I'm thinking of giving up the journalism apart from maybe some freelance stuff, and taking a long break in Tuscany so that I can just *write!*"

Of course he had always known that his "independence" would be backed ultimately by the security of his father's money. And it was becoming apparent that his wish to change his lifestyle was not founded on any deep dissatisfaction with himself. My hopes that he wished to resume analysis began to fade. But I needed to know more about his personal relationships, and this indeed seemed to be what he really wanted to talk about. He explained that when in Chile he had met an American woman – Cis, a journalist – with whom he had lived on and off for four years. "She was older than me. She had been there ever since the Allende government was toppled by the CIA and the massacres began. Even when I was back here, she was always going to and from South America. She was really committed. I admired her. She still sends me copy, though we haven't been lovers for a long time."

And then, Cis dismissed, he described how Ophelia had re-entered his thoughts after a chance encounter with her on leaving Polack's house in Cambridge after his visit.

"Remember how often I used to accuse you of being a romanticist?" he teased; "well now you'll say that I am one too."

His rather unctuous tone made me wary. But had we at last got to the reason for his requesting this consultation with me? He described how as he shut the front door he saw Ophelia get out of her car and usher two small children towards the house. "She's had her hair cut short, and she had her back to me, but I knew immediately it was her. It was like that other time – you remember – in the Market, after she came out of hospital. I could see she looked startled, but she was quite friendly. We said a few things – then…" Here Hamlet hesitated awkwardly, before forcing himself to say: "The thing was, when she said goodbye, she touched my hand for a second. I felt as though an electric shock was going through me. It made my hand burn."

He raised his hand slightly and looked at it, as if he half expected the stigma to be visible. I suggested he had been rather bowled over by actually seeing Ophelia again, presumably for the first time since leaving Cambridge, and he agreed. This pleased and encouraged me. Polack had told him, amongst other things, that Ophelia had not had an abortion but a miscarriage all those years ago ("so you see, she never actually got rid of my kid, not on purpose"), and that she was in the process of getting divorced from her husband. But it was seeing her and being struck anew by her beauty which revived his interest, together with the touch which he took as an invitation to intimacy. "It was then I really regretted how I'd thrown her away", he concluded.

I asked if he thought Polack had engineered this chance encounter.

"Oh, Polly!" he said wearily, with disdain. "Maybe – who knows, who cares? He's never liked John, of course. My mother didn't either – said he's always been too obsessed with his civil service career to be much of a family man. But Polly knows nothing about women and what they really want – he lives with his head in the clouds. I reckon the only time he ever had an affair was with my mother, years ago. They'd both deny it of course, but anyone could see they were in each other's pockets – but what did that teach him? Nothing. He just hasn't got it in him. I mean, she's free and available now, but you can see he wouldn't have the energy to go after her."

So his motive in visiting Polack was less to make up for his father, and more to arrange a suitable, safe consort for his mother. It was he who was the engineer. And annoyed, presumably because his mission had failed – this would lead him to denigrate Polack. *Hoist on his own petard.*

"Polly's basically a loner, you see", he continued. "He enjoys his retirement, hidden away from the world. He's got his study and his books and his college dinners – that's his life, he'll never reach out. *A poor cell.* My mother's not like that. She's as cultured as he is in her way – she reads everything – but for her that is secondary to a relationship. Polly just wouldn't know what a woman wanted from him. If he ever did. He'd never do for her now." *Nothing but a sot outside his books.*

Doubtless, I thought, Polack would not "do". I was conscious of a slight throb of excitement at the thought that Gertrude, rich and beautiful as she was, was indeed available. And I was aware that this account was Hamlet's way of offering her to me. What, I wondered suspiciously, might he have found out, or Gertrude perhaps hinted, about myself and Beatrice? But no, his previous curiosity about me as a transference figure seemed to have melted into thin air. Coming back to earth myself, I rebuked him for assuming it was his duty, now his father was dead, to marry off his mother.

"But don't you see, Dr Horacio", he said eagerly (as though we were now really talking business), "how useless Polly has become. That and my father's death – means it all lands up on my shoulders. Really, there's no-one else. Ophelia too – now that I know what I know about her situation, it's obvious Polly won't be able to help her." *And I the patient log-man.*

He believed Ophelia was unable to handle her divorce? I questioned, doubtfully.

"It's the psychological aspects I'm referring to", he explained insinuatingly. "Ophelia suffers from instability. I can tell you (and this is before anything I got from Polly) she used to sleep around indiscriminately, before her marriage to that tedious stick of a civil servant (and that didn't last long). When she was travelling around with her Early Music Consort, they used to swap partners as often as they swopped instruments. Everyone used to joke about it. *Good night, ladies, good night.* So now, with those two children as well, she's obviously in a very vulnerable position – prey to anybody who might want to pick her up."

I repeated that with his familiar omnipotence he was treating both his mother and Ophelia as helpless dependants whom it was his duty to accommodate – with the provision of trustworthy partners or perhaps, in the case of Ophelia, an analyst. ("Well somebody has to take responsibility", said Hamlet in an injured tone.) At the back of my mind, however, I found I was indeed wondering whether I could fulfil any of these roles which he figured forth so tantalizingly. My old romantic anxiety and protectiveness was revived. If Hamlet had really not returned with a view to more analysis for himself, would it not in fact be possible for me to take Ophelia in analysis? For some moments these temptations revolved in my mind as real possibilities. Only at the next stage of the interview did I come to my senses.

For Hamlet now mentioned almost casually, that he was considering inviting Ophelia to join him in Tuscany. "It would be a good break for her", he suggested. "And financially, everything is taken care of. My only problem is to make sure my mother's well settled before I go."

At last it fell into place. He was hoping to shelve the responsibility of his mother onto somebody else, so that with a clear conscience and plenty of money he could tempt Ophelia to go off with him. And I was supposed to be an accomplice in this.

I recognized now an effect which Hamlet had always tended to have on me. The possibilities he had conjured to my view excited my desire to step in and interfere beyond the bounds of my own countertransference to him alone – to add to the "heady mix" my own problems, memories and desires. Now this excitement turned to resentment, and anger at my foolishness in falling for his unctuous politic persuasiveness. Here again, I told him, was Hamlet the director of other people – especially the women in his life. In the old refrain, *reform it altogether.*

"But why shouldn't Ophelia join me out there?" he complained with mild irritation. "It would be a good place for her – I've got contacts there, someone who runs a music festival for example." *Sweet sounds that give delight and hurt not.*

His father's money, I accused him, had endowed him with a new flush of power. Now he was really acting the prince. He believed he could dispose of his mother in some secure, companionable relationship while he scooped off the princess and decamped to the pleasure ground. (I was furious at his crass attempt to enlist my services over Gertrude, in this context.)

"I know what you're thinking", said he, obtusely: "you're thinking, how will I cope with maintaining another man's kids, especially given Ophelia's history – isn't that a bit hard on the old ego? Well I've thought about it and I know I can do it. I've changed a lot since those days. In fact I quite like the idea of being a pater familias – we'll have our own as well of course. You could look on it as a good opportunity for exploring the roles of nature and nurture. And Polly would be pleased – he never liked her husband – too much of a career man, and not the kind of career that interested Polly either, so he felt an outsider." *He lost his daughter in that last tempest.*

Angrily, I demonstrated how his old grandiosity – hard and intractable – was here simply taking a new soft form. He now saw his role as "doing good" – having jumped onto the moral high ground to disguise his egocentric manipulations. Here was his old familiar sanctimony. *Reform, reform it altogether.* It was the same as his journalism, I told him, but applied to intimate relationships instead of social structures. Now that he had inherited his father's kingdom (in which – I stressed again – the decisive feature was the money) he seemed to feel these antics were justified. Was this the way to repair his relationship with his parents?

"All right", he said, as if deciding to play the card which he was sure would convince me of his sincerity, "there are psychological reasons too. You see, Dr Horacio, I'm quite convinced that if I did take Ophelia to Tuscany it would release my creativity. I know it's gone under with all this hackwork and the strain of having to earn my living. You must agree it would be a good thing if I got out of this hole."

But this of course seemed to me the final straw. Now, I said, he saw his inheritance as absolving him from working for the rest of his life. His phantasy of possessing Ophelia as a sort of magic talisman to release his creativity, in some idealized poetic retreat, was just his old omnipotence in a new guise.

"Have you considered, Dr Horacio", he insisted earnestly, adopting his serious interviewer's tone, "how it would benefit Ophelia to come with me? For her it would mean security – and I don't mean financial – I mean she'd be in no danger of slipping back into her old problems."

By now his complacency and arrogance were really getting under my skin. What was this, some mutual protection scheme to be imposed on Ophelia, some emotional life insurance? Could he not see the contempt for her that it implied? More than this (I finally demanded), had he considered the damage he had himself done his "creativity" when he had prematurely broken off his analysis all those years before? Until he came to terms with that, there was no hope of regaining it.

He seemed surprised that I should look at it in that light, and muttered furtively that he'd "never believed in hanging on in squeezed-out situations. I'm a mover, I knew it was time to go."
I jumped on board a pirate ship.

Well now, I said, the time had come, for him to tell me the truth about why he had run away from me all those years before.

"I didn't run away", he said petulantly. "I knew you'd done what you could for me ... and I *was* grateful – I wrote and told you, remember?"

Yes, I remembered his nasty letter well enough, I told him: a transparent piece of insincere rhetoric. I was the one he felt he had "squeezed out" and cheated. And now he expected absolution from his offence, for assurances to the effect that he had neither hurt me nor hurt himself. No, I said, it wasn't good enough; this time I really wanted to know the truth.

"What truth?" he muttered evasively.

The truth about what he didn't tell me at the time he left.

There was a period of silence. He sulked. The emanations from his mounting anxiety filled the room. *There was a beating about my heart.* Then he began:

"There was, I suppose, a dream I didn't tell you. It seemed like no big deal at the time. I knew exactly what you'd say about it, anyway. The funny thing is, it keeps coming back to me. Do you suppose there really is a repetition compulsion? It would be interesting to make that a topic for a piece or even a book, if one could only collect enough material from different people, preferably cutting across class barriers, to get at the archetypal –"

No! I interrupted. I was not to be deflected that easily, and time was running out. After eight years in the crows' nest I did not intend to lose sight of land once it hove in view. What was the dream? I insisted. He lifted his hands, shrugged, pouted, and began.

"*I was in the middle of a dark wood. It seemed both strange, and familiar. On one level I knew in the dream that I was in a particular place on the Heath* – I could show you the exact spot – *where there is a deep hollow with some huge old trees, and in the middle an oak tree which my father once told me was said to be 400 years old. That tree was a sapling in Shakespeare's day,* he said. *Beyond the hollow there is quite a wild bit with dense thickets* – you'd have to know the way in.

"Anyway – in the dream, *at first I was playing hide and seek with my friends. It was a child's game of course but we were grown up, our actual age – Ros, Gil, Nando, the usual crowd. At the same time it seemed we were in the middle of a jungle; there were strange cries and noises going on all around, in the treetops and thickets. That seemed to be quite natural, too; and I was having fun imitating some of the animal noises so that no-one could find me. Then I got fed up because they really didn't seem able to see me, the idiots, and*

I stepped out from behind the giant oak with my arms outstretched and yelled 'Here I am – Hamlet the Dane!'

"They stopped dead in their tracks and stared at me with utter imbecilic stupefaction. 'O Hamlet!' Nando finally mouthed, 'You've been translated!' They looked as though they'd been transfixed by the Medusa. As soon as they regained the use of their legs they scarpered away through the bushes, tripping over the brambles. 'Come back Nando you ass-head!' I called, but he only glanced at me again and ran. I decided to wait; I knew they'd be back. I lay down on a heap of leaves and looked up through the branches to the clouds overhead.

> "The odds are gone, I thought; the invisible worm
> Has bitten me too, the bite which means that boys and girls
> Are level with men no longer. Here I am,
> Yet cannot hold this visible familiar shape,
> Any more than a cloud, when through the leaves
> It presses on my branched thoughts, and alters
> The shape and texture of my head. The rack dislimns
> And makes me indistinct. The ass's ears are black
> Against the visiting moon, Ophelia's
> Dazzling canopy of hair like twigs and leaves
> Enfolds me pinioned so I cannot move,
> I cannot hear the words, the meaning ..."

"And then", said Hamlet, drymouthed, his words sticking in his throat, "I realized why she was smiling. The sides of my face were all hairy, and I could feel my ears were swollen and enormous. I was a monster – and she was laughing at me for looking such a fool!"

So this was it: the Selected Dream – the selected fact that unites the whole into an intelligible aesthetic pattern. *Bottom's dream.* How the devil had he come to have such a good dream? I was almost envious, wishing that dream had been mine.

Hamlet seemed nonplussed by my enthusiasm, in fact to find it rather distasteful.

"It was unpleasant enough at the time", he said sternly, "but it's nothing, is it, in cold daylight?'

At last it was clear to me why he had abandoned his analysis – what emotional commitment he found himself unable to face.

"So - what was it I couldn't face?" he reacted sarcastically. "It's just another dream about the Mousetrap fiasco – didn't I grovel over that sufficiently to meet your exacting standards?"

It was typical of him to assume the dream was about his humiliation, I said – about making an ass of himself through his directorship of the play. But here, he felt that the possibility of falling in love would make him look a fool in front of his friends, exchanging his familiar identity, Hamlet the Dane, for something watery and unclear. *The pendent boughs her crownet weeds clambering to hang.* Nothing could be more ridiculous. Not only this but also the meaning of words had become confusing in a way antipathetical to his characteristic control. *Her unshaped thought.* No wonder he had run away from an analysis which led him into disturbing situations, threatening so severely to undermine his status quo.

But Hamlet even now did not appear to take in my interpretation. He still could not confront the emotional implications of the dream. Instead his manner became harder and more contemptuous. It made no difference now in any case, he announced, since all that was in the past, and as for the future, he had "come to a decision" about that.

What exactly did he mean by a "decision", I asked coldly, anticipating the answer.

"I'm taking Ophelia with me. As soon as the divorce is through we'll go."

Had he actually consulted Ophelia on the matter? it suddenly occurred to me.

"You met Ophelia, didn't you", said Hamlet, with just a trace of his old sharp perception. "I'm sure she'd respect your advice."

I was astonished that he could still be trying to engage me as some sort of mediator, or matchmaker, after all I had been saying about his anti-analytic manipulations. Who did he think I was?

"Of course, as regards all that sleeping around she was doing", he persisted, as though convinced that this tack (of enlisting my concern about Ophelia) was his most effective ploy, "I realize now, it was probably there all the time waiting to come out – considering that in a sense she had an abused childhood, being screwed by her brother all those years –"

Here I interrupted him, my memory painfully jogged by some unworked-through feature of the analysis. I recalled Hamlet's wild accusation at the height of his Mousetrap mania, and repeated the question I had asked him then: what evidence did he have for this assertion?

"Evidence?" he exclaimed cynically. "Why, I've known for years. I told you before. Nando told me himself – when we were in India. And a lot of other things I didn't know. I was very gauche and ignorant then. I remember how surprised I was at first, in fact I didn't credit it at the time – he was always boasting – but later I put two and two together and the picture fitted. These days of course no-one would bat an eyelid ."

He talked on, but I had ceased to listen. The swine! I was thinking (remembering Ophelia's own account of her virginity) – Nando, the lying bastard! That was precisely the type of idea to have inflamed Hamlet's sanctimonious narcissism: encouraging him to assume that Ophelia was available for rescuing. If only I had had a clearer picture then of Nando's character, I thought, I could surely have rescued Hamlet from his clutches; or, if only Hamlet had been frank with me at that time (but that of course was our perennial obstacle). And then again, I found I was taking Nando's treachery personally, as if his desire to wreck Hamlet's relationship with Ophelia were directed ultimately at me, and was it true, that I was ultimately more interested in Ophelia anyway …

And now Hamlet was leaving, speaking some polite phrases, having regained his composed, ex-public-school demeanour. *Since no man, of aught he leaves, knows aught, what is't to leave betimes? Let be.* Both of us knew our meeting again would be fruitless.

"Good luck, Dr Horacio", he said, this time looking me in the eye, as if graciously accepting defeat in some sporting event. No, I thought, *I* am the one who has lost this game. I remembered the "blue sky" of his Winter's Tale session. Had I, even then, been over-optimistic? Was his longing for the unattainable blue sky a feature of his claustrophobia, rather than an anticipation of release? The depth of the tragedy, its full enormity, only revealed itself to me now, when I understood that Hamlet was truly lost;

my hidden half-conscious hopes for his return had survived until this meeting extinguished them for ever.

For the last time we shook hands, and I realized mine were trembling. Some horrible truth, or coalescence of truths, was beginning to impinge on my consciousness. I went next door for a cigarette, at the same time thrusting *Where Are We Now?* to the back of the bookcase. I would never read this banal caricature of what was once the heart of Hamlet's mystery. *So cracks a noble heart.*

Oh Absalom, Absalom!

CHAPTER ELEVEN

Horacio Agoniztes

> **Hamlet**:　　　　For thou hast been
> As one, in suff'ring all, that suffers nothing,
> A man that Fortune's buffets and rewards
> Hast ta'en with equal thanks; and blest are those
> Whose blood and judgement are so well commeddled
> That they are not a pipe for Fortune's finger
> To sound what stop she please. (III. ii. 65-71)

Horacio's dream of Gertrude and of Ophelia pulls together strands from his personal life and from Hamlet's analysis. Accepting their mutual interference at last, the "old romantic" is ready to review his own story.

On Saturday evening, after the meeting with Hamlet, I took my two daughters and their boyfriends to an expensive restaurant in Church Row to celebrate my fiftieth birthday.

Both the boyfriends were eminently unsuitable in my view, though nobody had asked my opinion, so I did not give it. My elder daughter, Antigone, a slender straight-backed girl resembling her mother, has a degree in Oriental Studies and an insatiable wanderlust which seems closely linked to the transitoriness of her amatory affairs. Her boyfriend of the hour was a wellbuilt but in no other way well-endowed youth whom she had picked up on the A40 when she had stopped to help him change the wheel on his car. He was on the dole but claimed he was seriously thinking of setting up a second-hand car sales business after this affecting incident – at least, that was how Antigone interpreted to the rest of the company his disconnected monosyllabic grunts and grins. My younger daughter Ismene, a sweet-natured girl, still a student, brought with her an unfortunately too-steady partner in the form of a young but wizened philosophy lecturer with restless paranoid eyes, whose capacity for ceaseless gabble would have made Hamlet – by contrast – look like a Zen Buddhist in the silent depths of contemplation. Ismene both idolized and mothered him, and he received both services complacently. As I watched the meaningless torrent of words catapulting from his mouth, swathed in a sleeve of microscopic food particles, I wondered what I had done to deserve this suffering. Yes, I thought, I am a man more sinned against than sinning.

Ever since the meeting with Hamlet I had been haunted by the wreckage of his youthful promise. Now, as I looked at Antigone and Ismene, it was Ophelia who came to the forefront of my mind, and a picture began to form of her present condition and situation. I could imagine vividly how she was now, eight years after I had last seen her, and the likely problems and complexities of her marriage and divorce. Observing my own daughters in this context, I puzzled over the perversities of the next wave of adolescents. Would they, I wondered, succeed in contracting even the type of conventionally unhappy marriage which Ophelia had made? A marriage which was at least appropriate in terms of class, looks, intelligence. Or was this the example they were studiously avoiding – a marriage which to the casual acquaintance appeared harmonious, though it was a torture chamber within? Certainly nobody could accuse my daughters' liaisons from even appearing well-matched from the outside. That was obvious to anyone – take the waiter for example (I observed):

"Allow me, sir", he was saying, ironically, as he placed a new tablecloth over the area in front of Wellbuilt, where the latter had spilt a glass of red wine. Solicitously, Ismene wiped the front of Wizened's jacket where it was splashed with crimson drops. To do him justice, Wizened had never stopped speaking, and appeared to ignore her ministrations. Wellbuilt grunted loudly at Antigone, who interpreted for him:

"Could we have another glass", she said. The waiter produced a new glass from behind his back and polished it, then placed it with a flourish on the mat.

"I mean, a different type of glass", said Antigone.

"It is a wine glass, madam", said the waiter, raising his eyebrows in mockery and speaking in a synthetically wounded tone.

"Could you bring a beer glass, please", she insisted defiantly, staring him in the eye. So a beer glass was brought for Wellbuilt.

Why on earth did I bring them here? I thought. Was this my punishment for marital failure? In fact Beatrice had only recently left me, to live with her lover of many years" standing; and the girls would be considered grown up by any normal standards. I found myself wondering how they would have behaved if Gertrude had been there. Gradually, my senses shut themselves against the inconsequential clatter going on around me. Wizened and Wellbuilt faded into the dim light of actuality and instead *I was seated at a small table opposite Gertrude, candlelit as once many years ago, but this time alone with her, drinking deep from her eyes and enveloped in her attentiveness to our mutual interests and desires.*

"You see, David," she was explaining, "I've always looked on myself as a type of surrogate mother to Ophelia. But it's been difficult, because I've never felt able to allow myself the direct influence that I could have had if she were legitimately my daughter."

"Sometimes that's the best way", I replied, thinking of my lack of influence on my own. But she, of course, interpreted my comment otherwise:

"Ah! you're thinking of Claude and Hamlet", she sighed softly. "The saddest thing is, how similar they really were underneath. They should have been friends. I always hoped they would be, one day

- but now it's too late. Have you noticed that Hamlet is even beginning to look a bit like Claude? He did when he was a baby, too, before his hair went straight. No", she said ruminatively, as though this thought had only just occurred to her, "I don't think Claude ever suffered from the delusion that Hamlet wasn't his. That was never part of his dissatisfaction. Hamlet was much more civilized towards him latterly, of course. But it was only a facade. You could see that in his heart, he still regarded his father as a bully of some kind, a dictator. And yet Claude was the gentlest of men! He never punished Hamlet in his life. I was the one who spanked him when he was naughty, when he was little."

Temperamentally, I observed, not for the first time, Hamlet was probably much more like his mother. A glass to see the inmost part of the other.

"Little and fierce!" she laughed. "But the truth is, David, I know he hasn't been happy, in the deep sense, all these years - and it's time he sorted himself out and found a permanent relationship. There are plenty of women who would have him, but he always seems to lose interest as soon as it gets serious – yet he's not a philanderer, he's just somehow – distractable. He doesn't seem to see the point of committing himself further. I've been worrying that he could become quite misanthropic. But it's Ophelia I really meant to talk about. I know, David, you'll understand what is in my mind: is there any chance, do you think, that they might be brought together again?"

I frowned, and shook my head sadly in shame and bitter frustration. I could not find any words to express my despair at what Hamlet had become, and at what Ophelia had become in his eyes. Gertrude gave me a sharp glance and explained,

"You see, I'm not sure she really understands the difficult situation she will be in, with the children - Antony is four, and Miranda is only two."

"She seems to be the one who's initiating it ... "

"John's not contesting it, he'd find that too degrading. From that point of view it will be straightforward."

"These things are always messy. But there is no point her wasting her life in an unhappy marriage like that."

"John is not a bad man. Just too distant, and – ambitious. He's not unlike Nando in some ways." Of unimproved mettle, hot and full.

"He's not right for Ophelia", I declared unequivocally. "It will be worse later on when he gets really stuck into his career at the Treasury. It's probably better for them to break it off now."

"So you don't think it would have been better to hold the family together, at least officially, until the children are grown up?"

"When are children ever grown up?" I said despondently. Gertrude looked at me in some surprise. Reproaching myself for having allowed my own filial troubles to surface yet again, I remarked that Ophelia's children were similar in age to herself and Nando when their mother died. That, agreed Gertrude, was what seemed to worry Ophelia most: repeating their family history of single-parentage.

"And the problem is, both the children are attached to their father", she continued. "In fact the less they see of him – since he's at work or away more and more – the more hysterical they get about demanding his company. John just couldn't take it. He used to idolize the little boy at first. It was as though he'd duplicated himself and proved his potency to the world, his image in miniature. But after Miranda was born, he went off Antony as well. Ophelia once said to me he never seemed to think of Miranda as his. And of course Antony was being impossible; it was only natural, he was jealous. But John couldn't seem to understand that. He took it as if it was an attack on him. The more tyrannical Antony got, the more cold and distant John became – with all of them."

Ophelia's description suggested to me a not uncommon narcissistic pattern amongst the type of men who were really big boys and had a limited tolerance of real children, beyond the point where they could be regarded as attributes of themselves. It did, of course, take two to make a marriage fail. I knew that well enough. But John seemed to retreat from the new turbulence aroused in him, rather than seeking help in dealing with it. I did not think the prospects for improvement were good.

"It's interesting you should say that", said Gertrude with a note of sudden understanding. "Because that's how he treated Ophelia, as well, at first. As if he was to be congratulated on having got the prize, won the race in the face of all the competition. She was an attribute of his, too. Did you know", she asked me pointedly, "that Ophelia went through quite a promiscuous phase, after Hamlet? Not exactly getting her own back, but testing her power over men as it were."

"It was the humiliation of everyone thinking she'd got pregnant to make Hamlet marry her." (How resentful I felt that instead of coming back to me, Ophelia had engaged in that dubious method of self-assertion.)

"Yet even after all that, she got pregnant again!" said Gertrude.

"That was John's way of getting her to marry him."

"Do you think so? It was her choice not to use the pill."

"She'd have decided the pill was invented by men to avoid responsibility for sex", I suggested.

Gertrude laughed, then leaning towards me earnestly she continued: "At that period, you know, David, I did use to worry that she might become a bit hardened towards men. With all that sleeping around – it had a sort of dutiful, mechanical quality. It wasn't even experimentation, exactly." *The primrose path of dalliance treading.*

Yes, I thought, I remembered from long ago that self-defensive aspect of Ophelia which she herself had been anxious about. But I could detect few traces of this in my present picture of her. She appeared, to my mind, livelier and warmer, despite her worry about the divorce.

"It was having the children that changed her", said Gertrude, as if reading my thoughts. "She opened up a lot once she had the baby to concentrate on. I think she was relieved to find she could have a baby, you see – after the miscarriage." Gertrude looked at me meaningfully with her deep, expressive dark eyes. I found myself wondering how much older than me she was – possibly six or seven years.

Then we spoke of Ophelia's regret at allowing Hamlet to believe he had made her have an abortion, owing to her vengeful desire for him to feel guilty, to punish him. She had confessed to Gertrude, not so long ago, that if she had discussed things honestly with him, things might have been different between them.

"Hamlet punished himself", said Gertrude sadly. "Perhaps Ophelia was luckier. At the time she seemed to have more to suffer, but she also had a whole world of experiences to wake up to, after hiding away in her music for so long. Like the Sleeping Beauty."

"She does seem to have neglected her music a little", I said.

"Only since Miranda, really", said Gertrude on reflection. "She was very involved before that."

"I don't suppose John gave her much encouragement."

"Not once he'd got her, no. Though he was proud enough of her accomplishments at first; they were part of the prize he had won. She told me once that she had a horror of ending up like Natasha in War and Peace — singing only until she got the right husband, then having a brood of children and getting fat!"

Gertrude laughed merrily at this. She herself, I noted inwardly, did not have the type of figure that would ever get fat. She was neat and lithe. I smiled as I considered their opposite, almost complementary, types of beauty.

"Well she hasn't got the right husband yet", I announced. Immediately I wished I had checked myself. Who was I really talking about, I wondered. Gertrude? Ophelia? Myself? What sort of web had I become enmeshed in?

Noises and vibrations from the outside world were beginning to edge into my dream, though I tried to fend them off. My head spun, and in a sudden nightmare flash I saw Gertrude's figure slipping away from me like Eurydice into the underworld.

"Wait!" I called urgently. "Gertrude, wait …". But she had returned to the shadows, leaving me more dazed and confused than after the most difficult patient.

"Daddy, wake up! You're in an absolute *dream*."

It was the clear bell-like voice of Ismene. She tapped my arm accusingly. I became aware that the airwaves around my head were delivering messages of an unpleasantly arhythmic and distorted quality:

"Once the discourse of the Feminine, so long hermetically sealed from history, has been demarginalized from the metabolical signifying practices of imperial phallocentricity, and renegotiates its sociality with and against the cerebrational determinants which have hitherto absented it from the existing cultural repertoire of referential significations, a new trans-hermeneutic validation of its excitingly deviational status could substantially restage its figurations, thereby unmasking the metapsychobiological violence committed on everyday speech –"

It was the voice of Wizened. From the persistent glare of his irritable, nervous and yet pleading eyes in my direction, and the shower of vaporous particles wafting down on my plate, I surmised that he was speaking to me. *This lapwing runs away with the shell on his head.*

"What's he saying?" I asked Ismene.

"Oh Daddy, honestly!" she said reproachfully. "He's asking if you'll write him a reference."

"Oh yes of course, I suppose so", I agreed hurriedly, feeling guilty about my absence of attention; "why, is he out of a job too?"

"No, Daddy – this is for a *university* post. It's a new lectureship. In Universal Hermeneuticals. It's interdisciplinary. It would suit Stephen brilliantly, it's absolutely his thing."

Yes, I thought, concentrating on averting my eyes from Wizened's gaze, it probably would.

"Oh, ah –", I responded helplessly, knowing of course that I was beaten; "why should they take *my* word for it? It isn't my field at all."

"Dad-*dy*!" breathed Ismene firmly, in her no-nonsense tone. "It's your field more than anybody's, surely. Aren't you always saying it's time psychoanalysis forged links beyond medicine, with the other humanitarian disciplines, and consolidated its wider cultural status?"

I wondered whether Wizened-speak could be infectious, and if so was it venereally transmitted or was it in the particles?

"Ye-ah", began Wellbuilt with a stretched-out grunt. I saw, to my surprise, that he was about to venture into speech. Indeed, once on his own track, it appeared he could be as eloquent as Wizened. "Without me, David, you're losing out. With me, you've got the tax opportunities. Soon as we get our Enterprises off the ground – yours and mine –"

"What?" I exclaimed, stunned.

"You know, our partnership – David and Michael Enterprises, right?" he leered encouragingly. "Tig's idea – right, Tig?"

"You haven't been listening, have you Daddy", accused Antigone in her turn. "And you agreed it was a good idea. I told Mick you were complaining about VAT on psychoanalysis. He said the way out is to start a joint business with him –"

"How on earth does he make that out?" I said, astonished. "It would be purely nominal of course", explained my daughter. "It would be in addition to your practice – and Mick will have his car sales as well, if he gets the site in South End Green."

"That's right David", confirmed Wellbuilt. "You gotta know how to play the system. We link up and you can forget VAT. In business these days – every loss is a tax gain. It's the only way to see real money."

A gain for him, a loss for me, I thought. I wondered if Wellbuilt's hefty frame concealed a certain low cunning, but decided against overestimating his intelligence. To avoid further discussion I signalled for the bill. But before escape could be effected, Wizened insisted on confirming his newfound solidarity with the company, clearly more relaxed and cheerful now that his reference was secured.

"I agree with Mick absolutely", he piped in an eager whine. "We're all partners now. The days of reductionist disciplines are over and the era of postmodern softhumanism has begun." I noted with relief that the appalling obsequious, hunted look had subsided from his eyes. "After all', he added, squinting at me companionably, "I'm sure you're not a subscriber to the doctrine of talent, are you, David?" *Know you this waterfly?*

It was a wet and windy night when we emerged from the restaurant. We came in single file up the narrow basement passage, myself first. As I reached the top, the wind seized the belt of my raincoat and hitched it over a railing, so I paused and slipped my arm through the railing to disentangle it. At that moment the visionless but solid head of Wellbuilt, mounting from below, hit me in the small of the back. I staggered into a slippery mound of sodden leaves and dog excrement and fell sideways with my arm trapped, giving it an agonizing wrench. I heard the bone crack. Wellbuilt loomed passively above me, swaying in the wind like a towerblock.

"Get out the way you great git!" shouted Antigone as she elbowed him in the stomach and helped me to my feet. She drove me to the Royal Free, with Wellbuilt grunting repentantly (to give him the benefit of the doubt) in the back of the car.

It was the end of Wellbuilt, I imagined, but he probably wouldn't have lasted anyway. They never did. I knew that

Wizened would be a much stickier proposition to dislodge. No merely physical catastrophe would serve the purpose. Ismene had been the type of child who was always bringing wounded birds and savaged small mammals into the house. Wizened was one of them. Her somewhat self-idealizing mixture of stubbornness and motherliness could make her pathologically dependable. I wondered yet again whether Beatrice and I had done the right thing in staying together because of the children. How often she had accused me of working too hard, of not listening to her, becoming impossible to live with, obsessed with self-aggrandizement. Stung, yet adamant, I had always reacted as though she were jealous of my work – jealous in a personal way. Patiently I used to explain that the work required this intimate emotional involvement; nothing less would do. Even after she had gone, I felt she must have made some mistake. Only now did I seriously ask myself whether I had really neglected her needs? Or was it that my blindness over the breakdown of our marriage had affected the sincerity of my work?

Thoughts increasingly painful and disturbing were being relayed into my consciousness through the painful jolting of my arm in the car. "Old romantic, old romantic". Hamlet's taunt was again vivid in my mind. I glanced sideways at Antigone, her bright eyes glittering and her small determined jaw tilting slightly upwards as she swerved at speed between the rows of parked cars in the irregular narrow street, with a gap of a hair's-breadth. Her style of driving was alarming if (one trusted) competent. She loved emergencies and had not yet found a vocation which supplied her with enough of them. Old romantic, old romantic. Antigone was certainly no romantic. But was her obstinate, feminist hardness, which insisted she only come into contact with men of whom she could feel contemptuous, so very different from my own romanticism after all? Was it indeed so different from Hamlet's hard sanctimony?

As I nursed my arm in the casualty waiting room, I felt for the first time my own romanticism to be in itself a hard shell, defensive, moralistic, idealizing of women. This was not the faith of my father. Was it against this that Hamlet had redounded when he closed himself to me and recoiled into the hard shell of his grandiose Forte consciousness, a prince of modern society? Like his parents, I wanted him to become a prince of the new age: to rescue it from the oncoming rule of the Wizeneds and Wellbuilts who now crowded the floor in all their vulgarity. I had romantic ambitions for him; perhaps I bullied him with my own hopes, heralding him as the chosen one, a repository for my own desires. Was it because of this that when it came to the point, he had been unable to fall in love – to make the leap of faith that Kierkegaard had diagnosed, and that was required of him by all the forces of development? Had my urgency and importunity weakened him – and is this why he had slipped away, on tiptoe, out of my zone of influence? And was this urgency of mine, in its turn, a substitute for faith in my own marriage? If I had had faith, would I have stayed with Beatrice – was it I who had driven her away?

> You from the Polack wars, and you from England,
> Are here arrived, give order that these bodies
> High on a stage be placed to the view,
> And let me speak to th' yet unknowing world
> How these things came about. (V. ii. 377-381)

When I was summoned to the X-ray department, I insisted that Antigone leave me and go home (maintaining that I was sure to spend the night in the hospital). Much as I loved her, I could not tolerate her company for long – a fact that frequently saddened me. She was a hindrance to thought – worse, a hindrance to feeling – and at that hour in the anonymous hospital corridor the pain in my arm acted as a magnet to a host of emergent emotional facts thronging in upon me. Now it was Nando, with his cynical big-brother bragging. It was not Ophelia who had been much affected by this (she seemed to accept it as a matter of course) but Hamlet whom I believed to have been poisoned by it. Before I met Ophelia, I had seen no reason to disbelieve that those two had an incestuous relationship. Hamlet believed it, and through him, so did I. Despite my questioning him for evidence, he must have sensed that was just a formality. My too-close identification with him was at fault.

But now, thinking it over yet again as I sat at my circular table in the lamplight in the early hours of the morning, with the dog dozing at my feet and a deep quiet outside, I could find no trace of my initial anger at Nando. His bragging was all standard stuff, and it ceased to matter whether it were true or not, it was a red herring. Truth lay elsewhere. *Where truth is hid.* Indeed, despite her efforts to "get rid of" her virginity, it was clear that Ophelia considered herself a virgin until her first serious relationship, with Hamlet. And I imagined that even now, despite the events which had filled the last eight years, Ophelia might still hanker after the boy who had first brought her out of the "nunnery" and into the world. My anger at Nando was inappropriate. But only now could I see that my protectiveness toward Ophelia was also inappropriate, and had been throughout the analysis. Vividly a phantasy of the night before returned to me. It had struck me with the force of a revelation, as the X-ray machine was moved down towards me and the radiographer made a minute adjustment to the position of my arm. I must have groaned aloud, as I remember the radiographer commenting sympathetically, "It's pretty painful, I expect."

Perhaps, it had just occurred to me, it was in this very room, some sixteen or so years before, that a fair-haired pubertal girl had sat, with possibly an identical injury, and a broken toboggan into the bargain, in her fury and defiance of "the boys" and the prospect of her menarche. *Drowned in her own defence.* I could almost see the anxious bald head of her father hovering beyond the screen. But it wasn't Nando (any more than Wellbuilt) who had broken my arm; and indeed, he had not broken hers. Her position, like mine, was essentially self-inflicted. Only now, through this parallel, was I able to understand the extent to which I had lodged my own femininity in this girl on the threshold of womanhood. I had projected onto her that which I should have retained as part of myself. It was an impossible burden for Hamlet to bear. Instead of waiting for him to fall in love, I had tried to will him into it – to enact for me my own being-in-love. Had I not always been a little in love with both those women in his life – "always on the side of the women" as he used to accuse me?

This was a crucial factor in my bungling of the countertransference. My own weakness had devolved upon Hamlet, my own failure to contain the impact of his "romantic" self. I could not forget Hamlet's farewell glance at our last meeting. It seemed the only honest communication of the entire interview. And now I knew why his grandiose attempt to marry me off to his mother had irritated me so much - because it was in a sense a reflection of my own desire, and not only that, a reciprocation of my own faulty method in handling his relationships. He had not been wrong in his phantasy of who might suit me, just wrong in his omnipotent and condescending view of such a relationship. Over the years of no contact, this vestigial recognition of a fault in the emotional transference between us had rigidified in his mind, so that I had ended up in his eyes in the caricatural form of a marriagebroker. He had returned my mistake to me, grotesquely, writ large with hyperbole – but it was my mistake.

"*He's no longer the boy you were once in love with*", I said to the Ophelia in my mind; "*his egocentricity has closed in.*"

"*Aren't all men like that?*" she said, looking at me intently. I replied, "*No.*" The tragedy of Hamlet was that he had *not* changed, he had merely crystallized, fulfilling his predetermined social role. *Subject to his birth.* To change requires a leap of faith, abandoning egocentricity to the winds. I had failed to instil this capacity in him because I had failed in it myself. The analysis had left him untouched, because it was no analysis. Like the Prospero of his dreams, I had wanted to shape his internal prosperity for him, egocentrically, self-directed. I had not allowed his story to evolve, and followed where it led; I wanted to be his storyteller. Driven by urgency and anxiety and the unmetabolized shadow of my crumbling relationship with Beatrice, to which I had turned a blind eye for so long, I interfered with the psychoanalytic method, I tried to push it onwards. Intolerant of uncertainty, I had allowed my feelings to splurge out, beyond the boundaries of the analytic context, tainting the receptivity of the transference.

Heaven and earth in the cage of form – that was the old Chinese poet's definition of a poem. Hamlet's analysis had been no poem. *An artistic failure,* as one poet infamously put it. No, an analytic failure. Or can one consider a psychoanalysis a work of art? And its failure, I saw now, was more than a mistake: it was a breach of faith, faith in the psychoanalytic method. "If I had had faith, I would have stayed with Regine." Kierkegaard's phrase throbbed insistently, renewing its impact. At last I understood how those words applied to me. If I had had faith I would have stayed with the psychoanalytic method in all its beauty; I would have followed its emotional requirements through the transference and countertransference. My mind would have been alerted to the pitfalls of my pilgrimage. I would not have confusedly and dogmatically strayed beyond those poetic boundaries, whatever the emotional turbulence aroused within them, whatever the distractions imposed from outside them. It wasn't just the dinner with his parents, it wasn't just the meeting with Ophelia – both of which, at the time, I excused as necessary breaches of technique – it was everything, my entire involvement weakened by non-analytic feelings. Not initially perhaps, but insidiously, as my personal blindness persisted. However vulnerable my personal situation made me, had I stuck to the psychoanalytic method, I would not have found myself trapped in the net of inappropriate relationships – with Claude and Gertrude, with Ophelia – which had undermined Hamlet's trust in my obedience to his childish needs. Crass, vulgar, aggressive those needs may have presented themselves, even ruthless at times, but as his wonderful dreams kept showing me, the heart of mystery was there. And he did develop during the analysis; his dreams drew forth his promise (perhaps this too blinded me to the dangers), but my containment was inadequate. *If thou didst ever hold me in thy heart* ... But I refused to be mystified, I withdrew from the path of unknowing. *Things standing thus unknown* ... and those things, perhaps, forever unknown – the man Hamlet might have become. In this trial of psychoanalytic faith I had failed, and I had failed Hamlet – yes *I* did it, a pipe for Fortune's finger. But to know a man well is to know oneself; and in that I am, perhaps, one stage further advanced than I was when I first began to tell this story to the yet unknowing world of my own consciousness.

INDEX TO DREAMS

Hamlet's dreams

Batman dream 58, 66, 72, 82, 89, 105, 108, 117
Bottom's dream 25, 85, 185
Chocolate-box dream 48, 84
Ghost dream 4, 51, 65, 67, 71, 77, 82, 93, 120, 127, 131, 148
Grave dream 18, 94, 97, 113, 117, 122, 123, 135, 173
Mousetrap dream 10, 63, 81, 1013, 106, 108, 113, 119, 129, 186
Museum dream 83, 134
Prospero dream 9, 133, 201
Submarine dream 120, 129
Tempest dream 129
"To be or not to be" dream 75
Winter's Tale dream 122, 134, 187

Horacio's dreams

Dream of Gertrude 191
Dream of Ophelia 201

Ophelia's dream

Her mother's coffin 166